PUZZLED by the 80s 2

CROSSWORD BOOGALOO

by Steve Lee

CONTENTS

Crossword puzzles were made utilizing **Crossword Weaver**, a licensed
software product by Variety Games Inc (Orem, UT, USA).

We recognize that some titles, quotes, and designations mentioned herein are the property of their
trademark holder. We use them for identification purposes only. This is not an official publication.

Thanks to YOU for buying this book! Well, unless it was a gift. If that's the case, thanks
to your friend for buying this book and to you for having a cool friend. If it's not too much
trouble, please take a moment and hit us up with a review. The more reviews we get, the better
we show up in search results, and we really could use all the help we can get!

.

GENERAL KNOWLEDGE 1

solution on page 102

ACROSS

3 The first CD pressed in the United States was, appropriately enough, this album

5 1982 Peter O'Toole film "My Favorite _____"

8 Sports car with gull-wing doors, featured in "Back to the Future…" three years after the company filed for bankruptcy

9 Amusement Park location of "Jaws 3-D", which incidentally is a solid 60 miles from the ocean so that makes no damn sense.

11 1982's "Dead Men Don't Wear ______"

12 Country in which the first non-US Disney Park was opened in 1983

16 1983 US television film that depicted the days following a nuclear strike

17 In 1980, the 3M company rolled out this brand of "repositionable notes"

19 1980 Michael Caine film, "Dressed to _____"

20 The first band to have a video game made featuring their image

DOWN

1 This teamster boss, missing for seven years, was declared legally dead in 1982

2 1985 Tom Hanks film, "The Man with One ___ Shoe"

3 Played by character actor Tracey Walter, this "Batman" henchman was the Joker's "number one guy."

4 1982 Richard Pryor film "Some Kind of. ___"

6 Andre the Giant's "Princess Bride" character

7 Charity supergroup consisting of mainly British and Irish musicians; released 1984 hit "Do They Know It's Christmas?"

8 Nickelodeon's first game show, in which teams compete in trivia and messy stunts

10 Band featured in a 1989 film documenting their performance at the Rose Bowl (the 101st and final stop on that tour)

13 Sound-activated electrical switch that was released in 1984.

14 1985 concert that was held in Champaign, Illinois, to raise money for US farmers

15 1983 sci-fi fantasy film about a planet invaded by "the Beast" and his army of Slayers.

18 Short lived TV spin-off of "Alice"

3 ACTORS IN A MOVIE

Can you identify a movie based on three cast members? Put your answers in the grid on page 7.

ACROSS

6	Craig T. Nelson, Zelda Rubinstein, JoBeth Williams
8	John Cusack, Tim Robbins, Daphne Zuniga
10	Bill Paxton, Lance Henricksen, Adrian Pasdar
15	Kevin Costner, Amy Madigan, James Earl Jones
17	Meryl Streep, Kurt Russell, Cher
20	Tom Cruise, Val Kilmer, Kelly McGillis
21	Billy Crystal, Meg Ryan, Bruno Kirby
23	Kevin Bacon, Lori Singer, John Lithgow
25	Robin Williams, Ethan Hawke, Robert Sean Leonard
26	Angie Dickinson, Nancy Allen, Michael Caine
28	Heather Langencamp, Johnny Depp, Robert Englund
33	Corey Haim, Jason Patric, Kiefer Sutherland
35	Frank Langella, Courteney Cox, Dolph Lundgren
39	William Hurt, Kathleen Turner, Richard Crenna
40	Tom Cruise, Rebecca De Mornay, Curtis Armstrong
41	Michelle Pfeiffer, Matthew Broderick, Rutger Hauer
42	Robert Redford, Glenn Close, Robert Duvall
43	Morgan Freeman, Jessica Tandy, Dan Aykroyd

DOWN

1	Dustin Hoffman, Jessica Lange, Geena Davis
2	Emilio Estevez, Rob Lowe, Demi Moore
3	Zach Galligan, Phoebe Cates, Howie Mandel
4	Michael J. Fox, James Hampton, Susan Ursitti
5	Eddie Murphy, Judge Reinhold, John Ashton
7	Debra Winger, Shirley MacLaine, Jack Nicholson
9	Warren Beatty, Diana Keaton, Jack Nicholson
11	Kyle McLachlan, Dennis Hopper, Laura Dern
12	Peter Weller, Nancy Allen, Kurtwood Smith
13	Tom Cruise, Dustin Hoffman, Valeria Golina
14	Gene Wilder, Richard Pryor, Craig T. Nelson
16	Robin Williams, Bruno Kirby, Forest Whitaker
18	Matt Dillon, Kelly Lynch, Heather Graham
19	Rodney Dangerfield, Sally Kellerman, Sam Kinison
22	Tom Cruise, Mia Sara, Tim Curry
24	Mel Gibson, Danny Glover, Gary Busey
27	Drew Barrymore, George C. Scott, David Keith
29	Helena Bonham Carter, Julian Sands, Maggie Smith
30	Kevin Costner, Robert DeNiro, Sean Connery
31	Joan Severance, Kurt Fuller, Hulk Hogan
32	Meryl Streep, Kevin Kline, Peter MacNichol
34	Patrick Swayze, Jennifer Grey, Cynthia Rhodes
36	Robert DeNiro, Joe Pesci, Cathy Moriarty
37	Bruce Willis, Alan Rickman, Bonnie Bedelia
38	Bill Murray, Howard Ramis, John Candy

ACTORS IN A MOVIE 1

COMEDY MOVIES 1

solution on page 102

ACROSS

1 Mark Harmon stars as a gym teacher who is forced to teach remedial English

6 "The name in laughter from the hereafter"

7 Bette Midler plays a kidnapped wife, and Danny Devito is her husband who doesn't want her back.

8 After he's laid off, Michael Keaton becomes a stay-at-home dad.

9 Gene Wilder met his future wife whilst filming this 1982 comedy/thriller

13 This 1988 Steve Martin/Michael Caine comedy is a remake of 1964's Marlon Brando/David Niven film "Bedtime Story."

14 1984 supernatural comedy with Bill Murray

17 1983 comedy starring Dave Thomas and Rick Moranis as their SCTV characters, Bob and Doug McKenzie

18 Bruce Willis is the inner voice of Baby Mikey in a movie that inexplicably made *twice as much money* as "Die Hard."

19 This 1984 comedy pits a group of intellectuals against a jock fraternity. To say this one aged poorly would be quite an understatement.

DOWN

1 Molly Ringwald's family forgets her birthday, and it all rolls on from there.

2 John Cusack is a struggling artist who spends his summer with Demi Moore in Nantucket. I've had worse summers.

3 To escape a gambling debt, spoiled rich boy Tom Hanks joins the peace corps

4 Richard Dreyfuss and Danny Devito play feuding aluminum siding salesmen.

5 Michael Keaton convinces a Japanese auto company to take over a US plant

6 A wealthy businessman enrolls in college to inspire his distant son.

10 1980 film about the goings-on at the very exclusive Bushwood Country Club. Also something about a puppet rodent.

11 Minor league baseball players compete for the affections of a baseball groupie

12 Matthew Broderick enlists in this second film of Neil Simon's "Eugene Trilogy."

15 Arnold Schwarzenegger and Danny Devito play fraternal offspring. That's the joke.

16 A young boy makes a wish to be an adult. Ends up becoming Tom Hanks. Not bad.

GENERAL KNOWLEDGE 2

solution on page 102

ACROSS

1 1981 John Travolta thriller, based on Michelangelo Antonioni's 1966 film "Blowup"

7 1989 hurricane that thrashed South Carolina

8 1981 John Belushi romantic comedic drama, "Continental _______."

10 Clint Eastwood thriller where he must infiltrate Russia and steal a high-tech jet.

12 Oliver Stone 1986 film, the first in his trilogy of Vietnam War-themed movies.

15 Host city of the 1984 Summer Olympics

18 The first a capella song to reach number one on the Billboard Hot 100 chart was performed by Bobby _________.

19 1985 film features Roger Moore's seventh and final appearance as James Bond.

20 Debuting on April 12, 1981, this was the first of five space shuttles used by NASA.

DOWN

2 This 1981 sci-fi film, directed by Michael Crichton and starring Albert Finney, was the first to feature 3D computer shading. Too bad it was a stinker, huh?

3 James Caan film about a safecracker trying to go legit; director Michael Mann's first film.

4 Character played by Anthony Michael Hall in "The Breakfast Club," the brain.

5 This former actor became President of the United States on January 20, 1981

6 This villainous character wears a hockey mask throughout the film, and he did it in a movie *a year before* Jason did it.

9 This network launched as a competitor to the "big three" on October 9, 1986.

11 1988 song by Rob Base and DJ E-Z Rock that samples Lyn Collins' 1972 song "Think (About It)."

13 Daryl Hannah film based on a novel by Jean M. Auel, "The ____ of the Cave Bear"

14 Walter Mondale's 1984 running mate, she was the first female VP nominee.

16 Neil Simon's 1982 semi-autobiographical play, "Brighton Beach _______"

17 American female rap group that had a breakout hit with 1988's "Supersonic"

DRAMA TV SHOWS

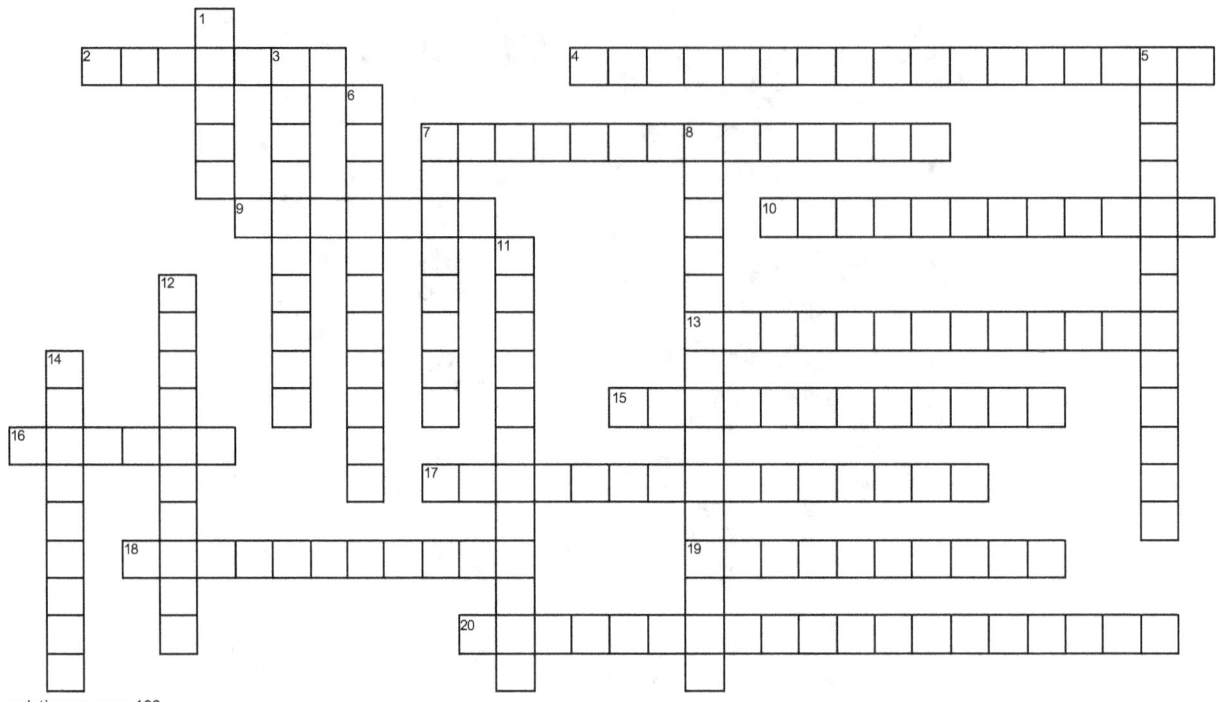

solution on page 102

ACROSS

2 Primetime soap about the trials and tribulations of the Carringtons

4 Fantasy/drama that followed the relationship of a man-beast and an assistant DA

7 Look, don't EVER go to Cabot Cove, Maine. People die there all the time, and the only person who can solve the murders is a mystery writer

9 Andy Griffith plays an Atlanta based defense lawyer who, much like Perry Mason, would ID and confront the real criminal in court

10 This spin-off of Dallas featured Joan Van Ark, Donna Mills, and Ted Shackelford.

13 This spin-off of M*A*S*H found Dr. John McIntyre working as chief of surgery at San Francisco Memorial Hospital

15 Edward Woodward plays a former intelligence agent who helps innocent folks who locate him through a classified ad.

16 This show's 1980 episode "Who Done It" was the second highest rated primetime telecast ever.

17 Michael Landon plays an angel sent to Earth in order to help people in need.

18 Dallas, but with wine instead of oil.

19 Starring Chris Burke, the first series to have a main character with Down Syndrome

20 Mississippi-set series with Carroll O'Connor, based on a 1965 novel and 1967 film:

DOWN

1 Harry Hamlin / Corbin Bernsen legal drama

3 Lee Majors plays a Hollywood stunt man who moonlights as a bounty hunter

5 Gerald McRaney and Jameson Parker play brothers who run a detective agency

6 Series about a teaching hospital; featured an ensemble cast including Howie Mandel, Denzel Washington, and Mark Harmon

7 Richard Dean Anderson plays a secret agent who can make damn near anything out of whatever crap is lying around.

8 Daniel J. Travanti led a large ensemble cast in this police procedural that was heavily influential in both its visual style and its serialized storytelling.

11 Cybil Shepherd is a former model who runs a detective agency with Bruce Willis

12 Medical drama set at an evacuation hospital during the Vietnam War.

14 South Florida-based crime drama that drew inspiration from New Wave culture.

NEW WAVE

Alright, this should be pretty simple. I give the song, you give the band.

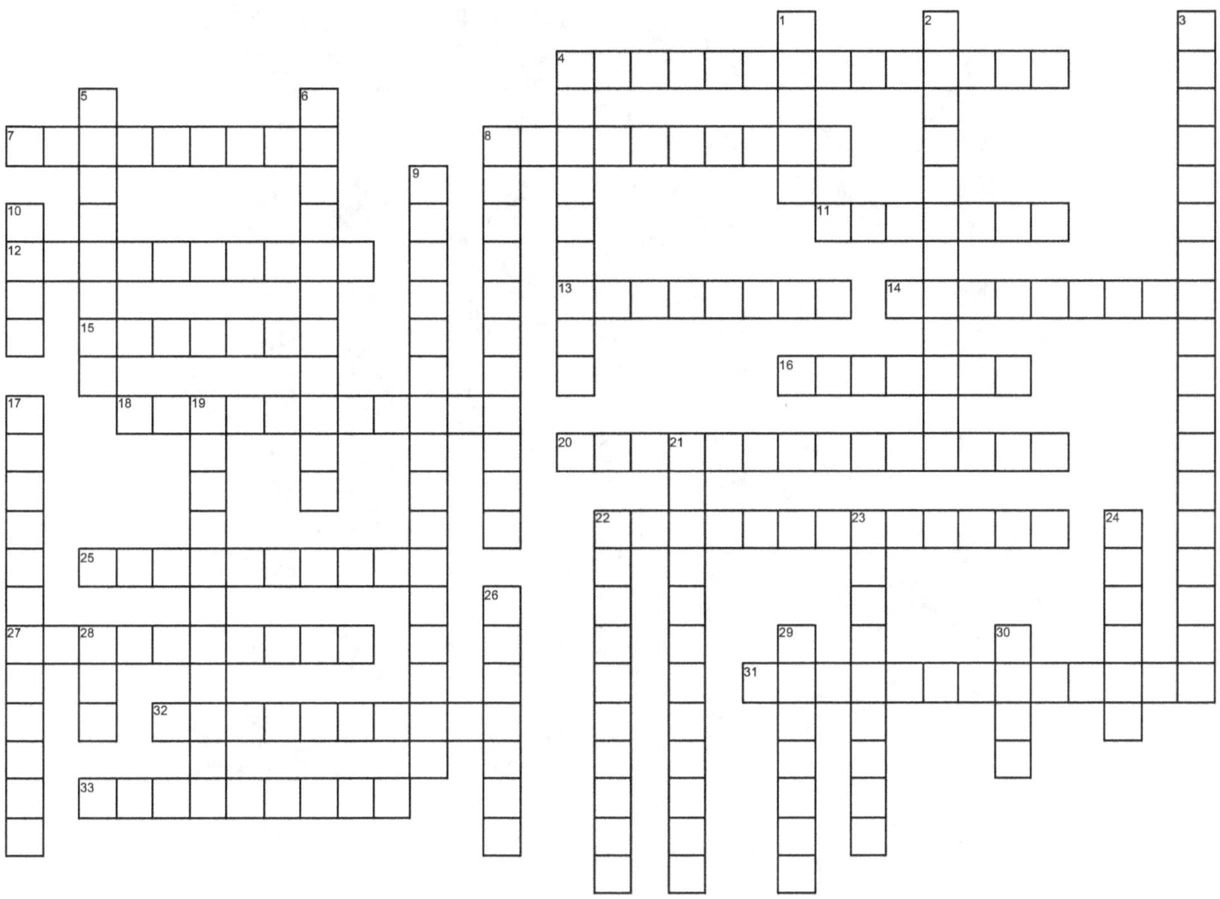

solution on page 103

<table>
<tr><td>

ACROSS

4	Human
7	Don't Stand So Close to Me
8	Breaking us in Two
11	Call Me
12	Sweet Dreams (Are Made of This)
13	Our Lips Are Sealed
14	Under the Milky Way
15	A Little Respect
16	You Might Think
18	It's a Sin
20	Walking in L.A.
22	Shout
25	Cruel Summer
27	Notorious
31	Hold Me Now
32	Forever Young
33	Cars

</td><td>

DOWN

1	Situation
2	Girlfriend is Better
3	Love My Way
4	How Soon is Now?
5	Blue Monday
6	Little 15
8	Love Will Tear Us Apart
9	Space Age Love Song
10	Whip It
17	Don't Dream It's Over
19	Hyperactive!
21	True
22	Voices Carry
23	More Than This
24	No More Words
25	Hourglass
28	The One I Love
29	Just Like Heaven
30	Never Tear Us Apart

</td></tr>
</table>

GENERAL KNOWLEDGE 3

solution on page 103

ACROSS

1 Jack Burton's "Big Trouble in Little China" rig was named the __________ Express

6 Surname of the singer who was elected mayor of Palm Springs in 1988.

7 The actual name of the Princess Bride

9 Chevy Chase gets telekinesis from exposure to nuclear waste in this 1981 comedy: "_______ Problems"

13 Actress/Singer who appeared as the public defender in season 2 of "Night Court;" also known for singing on Meat Loaf's "Paradise By the Dashboard Light"

15 Popular 80's fashion, _____-washed jeans

17 City that hosted the 1984 Winter Olympics

18 1981 German submarine war film that was a big success both critically and financially

20 Sleepy little New England town where Cher, Michelle Pfeiffer, and Susan Sarandon form a coven in a 1987 film.

21 1983 film with a group of college friends reuniting, "The Big _____"

DOWN

2 1981 Disney film starring Michael Crawford as a comic book writer who pretends to be his creation to help a KGB agent defect

3 Based on an SNL sketch, John Belushi and Dan Aykroyd are the _____ Brothers

4 Sarah Jessica Parker is an awkward high school girl trying to impress the popular girls in this short lived 1982 series.

5 1984 cult classic with Emilio Estevez, Harry Dean Stanton, and a 1964 Chevy Malibu with something weird in the trunk.

8 1981's "Omen III: The Final _________"

10 Nickname for the 1980s-era L.A. Lakers

11 Host city of the 1980 Winter Olympics

12 1981 John Waters film that satirized suburbia and was presented in "Odorama"

14 Critically panned but successful 1980 Brooke Shields film, "The Blue _______"

16 1982 black comedy with Paul Bartel and Mary Woronov as the Blands, "Eating _____"

19 Bruce Campbell's "Evil Dead" character

WHAT ALBUM?

Like the title says, I've given you the big song – you fill in the album that song was on.

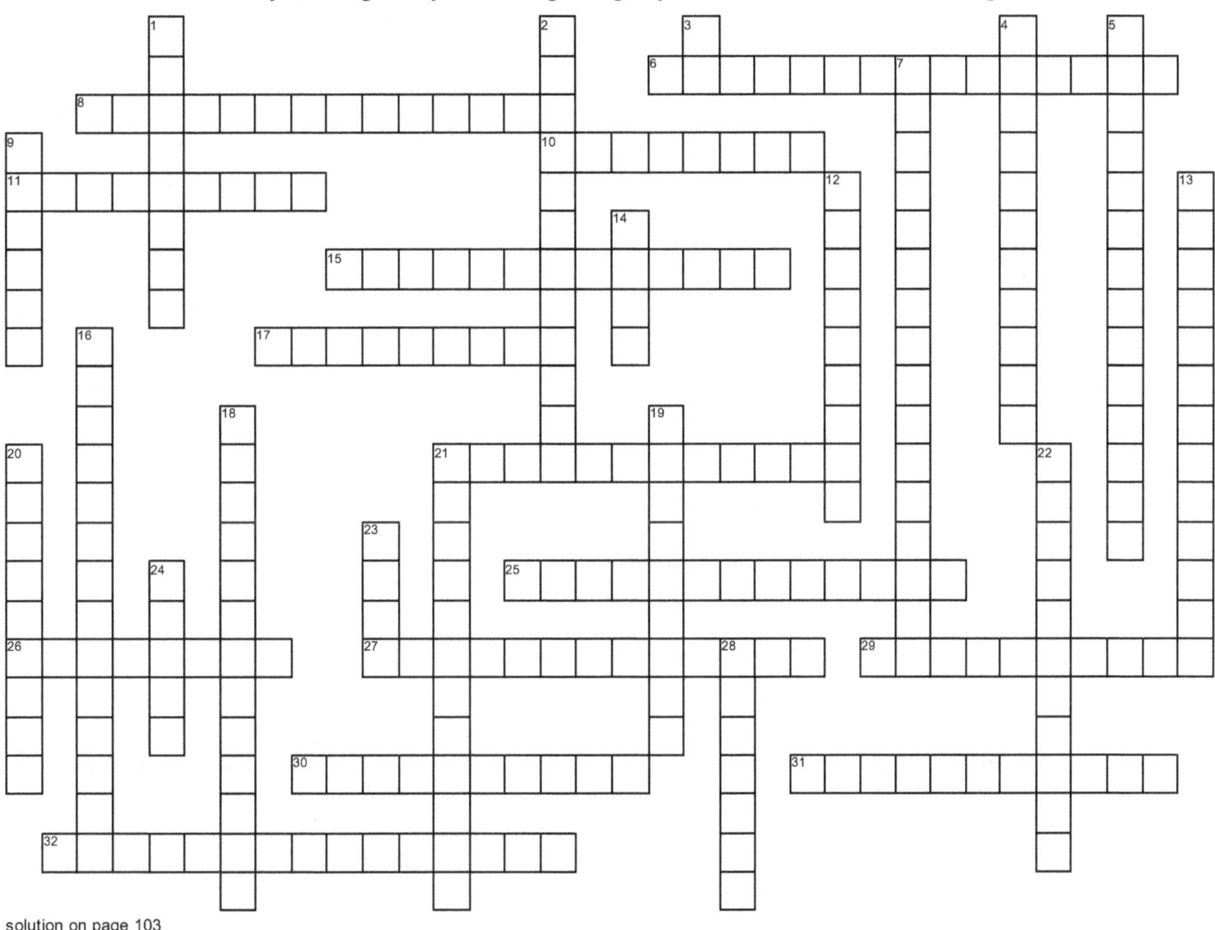

solution on page 103

ACROSS

6	People are People
8	Fascination Street
10	Wanna Be Startin' Something
11	R.O.C.K. in the U.S.A.
15	Every Breath You Take
17	You Can Call Me Al
21	Running Up That Hill
25	Girls Just Want to Have Fun
26	Hungry Heart
27	What's Love Got to Do with It?
29	Gimme All Your Lovin'
30	I Would Die 4 U
31	Express Yourself
32	Allentown

DOWN

1	Pour Some Sugar On Me
2	All Night Long
3	Sledgehammer
4	Cum on, Feel the Noize
5	Money for Nothing
7	Harvester of Sorrow
9	Open Arms
12	Bad Medicine
13	I Won't Back Down
14	Need You Tonight
16	In Too Deep
18	Brass Monkey
19	Listen to Your Heart
20	Careless Whisper
21	Keep On Loving You
22	You Shook Me All Night Long
23	Love in an Elevator
24	I Want Your Sex
28	What Have You Done for Me Lately?

ARCADE GAMES

solution on page 103

ACROSS

2 Vertical Scrolling Driving/Shooting game, inspired by James Bond films; uses the Peter Gunn theme for background music

4 1981 game where your character must cross the road and the river to get home.

6 1982 combat game where knights fight with lances while mounted on large birds

8 Popular 1986 driving game where players control a Ferrari Testarossa

9 Olympic themed game where players smash two buttons as quickly as possible to make their character go faster.

10 Action game known for switching perspectives (from side scroller to 3D); players play as commandos

12 1980 game where players control the "Bug Blaster" with a trackball

14 Players play as Peter Pepper, who must avoid enemies like fried eggs and pickles

18 1982 sequel to 12-across

20 Fixed shooter game that was a sequel to 1979's Galaxian

21 Interactive LaserDisc video game with animation by Don Bluth

22 Two-joystick game where players have to fight off waves of killer robots

DOWN

1 Players control Sir Arthur, who strives to rescue Princess Prin-Prin from Astaroth

2 1987 fighter with Ryu and Ken

3 1980 game where players defend six cities from an ICBM attack

5 4-player dungeon game, *needs food badly.*

7 Players play as Jumpman, trying to rescue Pauline from the titular gorilla

11 Players defend astronauts from attacking aliens in this game, considered to be the first side scroller.

13 Underground game where players defeat enemies by inflating them with air until they explode. Gruesome, right?

15 Players control one of three monsters trying to survive being attacked by military forces

16 Players ride a bike down the street delivering newspapers. Get a job!

17 Players clear stages by jumping from cube to cube until the whole board is the same color. Watch out for Coily!

19 The only arcade game that inspired both a top ten song and a Weird Al parody (utilizing the Beatles' "Tax Man")

ACTION MOVIES 1

solution on page 104

ACROSS

1 Olympic gymnast Kurt Thomas stars as a gymnast who combines gymnastics with martial arts.

4 Patrick Swayze and Liam Neeson play brothers out to avenge the murder of their younger brother (Bill Paxton).

8 Clint Eastwood is a former Air Force Major tasked to steal a Russian jet

12 Carl Weathers is a Detroit detective on the trail of a power-hungry auto magnate

14 Jon Voight and Eric Roberts are escaped convicts on an out-of-control train; based on a 1960 screenplay by Akira Kurosawa!?!

15 Rutger Hauer stars in this action film based on a Steve McQueen TV series

16 Sylvester Stallone and Billy Dee Williams are detectives out to get a group of international terrorists led by Rutger Hauer

17 1989 Jean-Claude Van Damme flick where he must fight his opponent in "the ancient way."

18 Burt Reynolds is a security guard who must protect Liza Minnelli

19 Ellen Ripley returns to LV-426, and she's got backup this time.

20 Sean Connery returns as James Bond in a second adaptation of "Thunderball"

DOWN

2 Schwarzenegger must fight to survive this futuristic game show

3 Sword and sorcery flick with Arnold Schwarzenegger and Brigitte Nielsen

5 Chuck Norris returns to Vietnam to rescue POWs in a blatant rip off of "Rambo." No, really! Look it up. They totally ripped it off and rushed it to theaters two months earlier.

6 Sylvester Stallone is a LA cop protecting Brigitte Nielsen from "The Night Slasher"

7 The fifth and final "Dirty Harry" movie

9 Dolph Lundgren is a Spetsnaz operative who joins a group of desert rebels and fights against Soviet forces

10 Ralph Macchio is a bullied teenager who is taught karate by handyman Pat Morita.

11 Sidney Poitier is an FBI agent who teams up with tracker Tom Berenger to pursue a murderer who is fleeing though the mountains

13 A professional "cooler" at a roadside bar protects locals from a corrupt businessman.

FIRST LINES – WHAT'S THAT SONG?

For this one, I'm giving you the first few lines of popular songs.
Fill in the grid on page 17 with the names of these songs.

ACROSS

2   Color me your color, baby. Color me your car. Color me your color, darling. I know who you are.

4   Been working so hard, I'm punching my card. Eight hours, for what? Oh, tell me what I got.

6   Hi there! I'm on my way, I'm making it. I've got to make it show, yeah.

14   Friday night I crashed your party. Saturday I said "I'm sorry" Sunday came and thrashed me out again.

17   Pressure pushing down on me, pressing down on you, no man ask for.

18   I'm in the dark, I'd like to read his mind. But I'm frightened of the things I might find.

22   I am the son, and the heir, of a shyness that is criminally vulgar

26   How does it feel to treat me like you do? You've laid your hands upon me and told me who you are.

27   I never meant to cause you any sorrow. I never meant to cause you any pain.

29   Oh baby don't it feel like heaven right now? Don't it feel like somethin' from a dream?

31   You with the sad eyes. Don't be discouraged, oh I realize.

33   Here in my car, I feel safest of all. I can lock all my doors, it's the only way to live in cars.

34   All the men come in these places, and the men are all the same.

35   I walked along the avenue. I never thought I'd meet a girl like you. Meet a girl like you.

37   Ah, watch out. You might get what you're after. Cool babies, strange but not a stranger

38   I believe the children are our future. Teach them well and let them lead the way

39   I feel the night explode when we're together, emotion overload in the heat of pleasure

DOWN

1   Close your eyes, give me your hand darling. Do you feel my heart beating? Do you understand?

3   Summer, it turns me upside down. Summer, summer, summer, it's like a merry-go-round

5   I wanted to be with you alone, and talk about the weather

7   Darken the city night is a wire. Steam in the subway, earth is afire

8   Caroline laughs and it's raining all day, she loves to be one of the girls

9   Don't think sorry's easily said. Don't try turning tables instead.

10   Lover, I'm off the streets. Gonna go where the bright lights and the big city meet

11   Another suburban family morning, Grandmother screaming at the wall

12   Well I guess it would be nice if I could touch your body. I know not everybody has got a body like you.

13   It's close to midnight, and something evil's lurking in the dark

15   I'm saying all the things that I know you'll like, making good conversation.

16   I don't know when to start or when to stop. My luck's like a button, I can't stop pushing it

19   "Show me, show me, show me how you do that trick. The one that makes me scream," she said

20   I'm lying alone with my head on the phone, thinking of you 'til it hurts

21   Standing in line, making time, waiting for the welfare dime 'cause they can't buy a job

23   Now, the mist across the window hides the lines but nothing hides the color of the lights that shine

24   Come over here. All you've got is this moment. Twenty-first century's yesterday.

25   Born down in a dead man's town, the first kick I took was when I hit the ground

28   Got me a movie, I want you to know. Slicing up eyeballs, I want you to know

30   I get up and nothin' gets me down. You got it tough, I've seen the toughest around

32   There'll be times, when my crimes, will seem almost unforgivable.

36   I've been alone with you inside my mind. And in my dreams I've kissed your lips a thousand times.

FIRST LINES – WHAT'S THAT SONG?

(Use the clues on the page 16)

solution on page 104

FIRST LINES – WAIT, BUT WHO DID THAT SONG?

You did a great job on the previous puzzle, so this one should be a cinch. Here's the same lyrics from before – just fill in the grid on page 19 with the band / artist that did the song!

ACROSS

1   Friday night I crashed your party. Saturday I said "I'm sorry" Sunday came and thrashed me out again.

9   Now, the mist across the window hides the lines but nothing hides the color of the lights that shine

10   Standing in line, making time, waiting for the welfare dime 'cause they can't buy a job

14   I'm lying alone with my head on the phone, thinking of you 'til it hurts

17   I believe the children are our future. Teach them well and let them lead the way

18   "Show me, show me, show me how you do that trick. The one that makes me scream," she said

19   Color me your color, baby. Color me your car. Color me your color, darling. I know who you are.

20   Summer, it turns me upside down. Summer, summer, summer, it's like a merry-go-round

22   I get up and nothin' gets me down. You got it tough, I've seen the toughest around

23   There'll be times, when my crimes, will seem almost unforgivable.

24   I walked along the avenue. I never thought I'd meet a girl like you. Meet a girl like you.

25   I wanted to be with you alone, and talk about the weather

29   Been working so hard, I'm punching my card. Eight hours, for what? Oh, tell me what I got.

31   Born down in a dead man's town, the first kick I took was when I hit the ground

32   Oh baby don't it feel like heaven right now? Don't it feel like somethin' from a dream?

34   Don't think sorry's easily said. Don't try turning tables instead.

35   I'm in the dark, I'd like to read his mind. But I'm frightened of the things I might find.

36   All the men come in these places, and the men are all the same.

37   How does it feel to treat me like you do? You've laid your hands upon me and told me who you are.

DOWN

2   I've been alone with you inside my mind. And in my dreams I've kissed your lips a thousand times.

3   Got me a movie, I want you to know. Slicing up eyeballs, I want you to know

4   Pressure pushing down on me, pressing down on you, no man ask for.

5   I don't know when to start or when to stop. My luck's like a button, I can't stop pushing it

6   Darken the city night is a wire. Steam in the subway, earth is afire

7   You with the sad eyes. Don't be discouraged, oh I realize.

8   I'm saying all the things that I know you'll like, making good conversation.

11   Ah, watch out. You might get what you're after. Cool babies, strange but not a stranger

12   It's close to midnight, and something evil's lurking in the dark

13   I never meant to cause you any sorrow. I never meant to cause you any pain.

15   Caroline laughs and it's raining all day, she loves to be one of the girls

16   Here in my car, I feel safest of all. I can lock all my doors, it's the only way to live in cars.

21   I feel the night explode when we're together, emotion overload in the heat of pleasure

25   I am the son, and the heir, of a shyness that is criminally vulgar

26   Another suburban family morning, Grandmother screaming at the wall

27   Well I guess it would be nice if I could touch your body. I know not everybody has got a body like you.

28   Close your eyes, give me your hand darling. Do you feel my heart beating? Do you understand?

30   Hi there! I'm on my way, I'm making it. I've got to make it show, yeah.

33   Come over here. All you've got is this moment. Twenty-first century's yesterday.

FIRST LINES – WAIT, BUT WHO DID THAT SONG?

(Use the clues on the page 18)

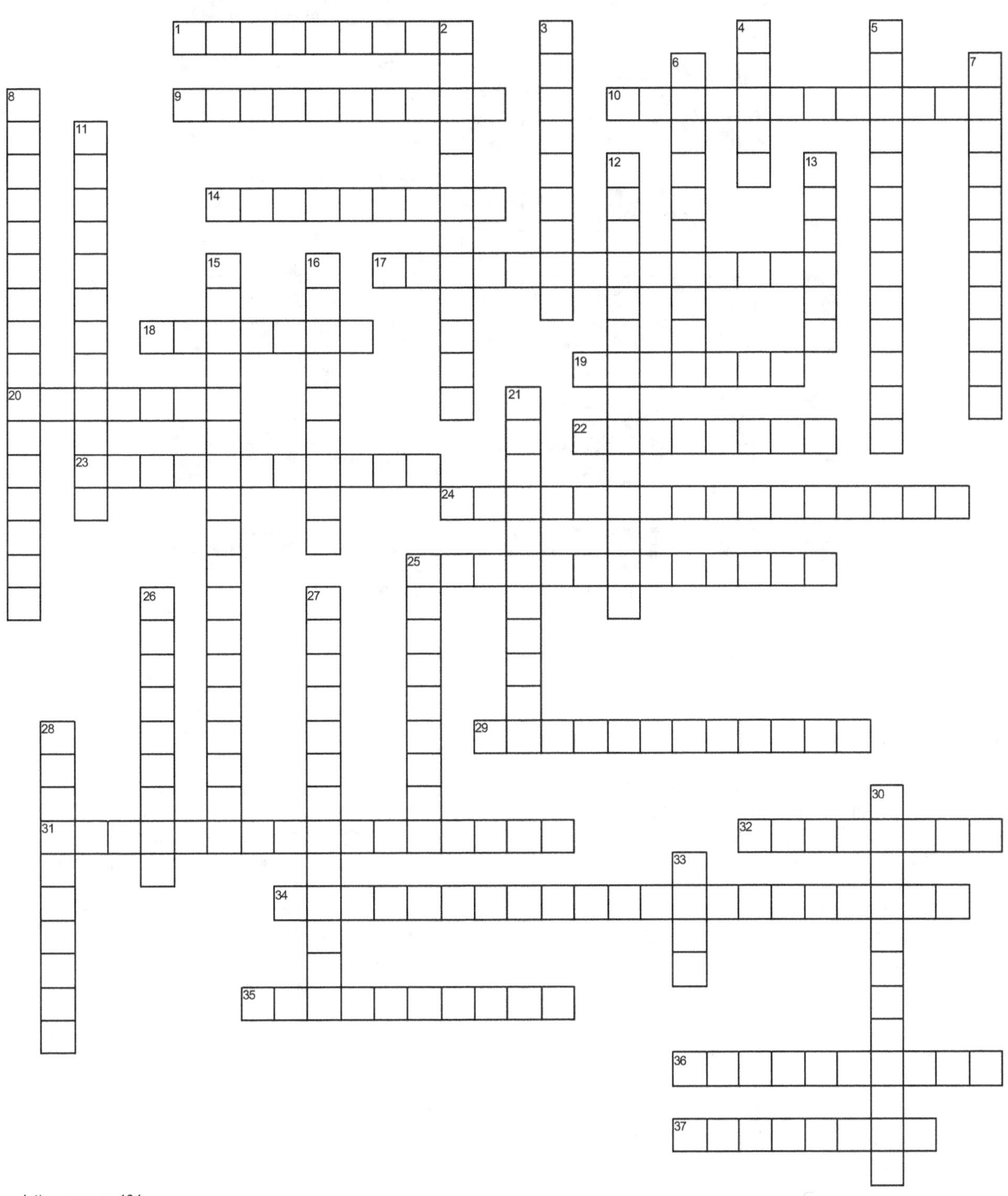

solution on page 104

GENERAL KNOWLEDGE 4

solution on page 104

ACROSS

2 1986 Rob Lowe hockey flick that was also Keanu Reeves' first film

4 Robert Redford's acclaimed 1980 directorial debut, "_______ People"

5 1985 biopic of Roy "Rocky" Dennis

8 A bioengineered human intended for working off-world in "Blade Runner"

9 This Bill Murray army comedy was originally intended for Cheech and Chong

10 According to the end titles of "Fast Times at Ridgemont High," Jeff Spicoli paid this band to perform at his birthday party

11 Chemical substance created by Judge Doom that destroys toons

14 Mythological character portrayed by Harry Hamlin in "Clash of the Titans"

15 Villainous Kryptonian General portrayed by Terence Stamp in "Superman 2"

17 Syndicated game show; revived in 1984

18 1980 Bette Davis film "The _______ in the Woods"

19 Horror film that featured the final roles of Fred Astaire and Douglas Fairbanks, Jr

20 1981 precursor to MS Windows

DOWN

1 Maverick's first Radar Intercept Officer

3 The final leader of the Soviet Union

5 Produced "The Elephant Man," but left his name out of the credits lest people think the movie was a spoof

6 Australian actor/singer who had a big hit with a cover of Little Eva's "Loco-Motion"

7 Queen's last US tour with Freddie Mercury was to promote this, their tenth album

8 Patrick Swayze rips out a dude's throat in this movie. What else do you need to know?

12 Aquatic creature that attacked the Goonies in a deleted scene (still referenced at the end)

13 1980 South African comedy, "The Gods Must Be ______."

16 Michel Biehn's colonial marine character in "Aliens," confused with Private Hudson.

SITCOMS

solution on page 105

ACROSS

2 Show that introduced America (for better or worse) to the Olsen Twins

5 Emmanuel Lewis plays a young boy who is adopted by his NFL-pro godfather

7 Ted Knight is a cartoonist in this show, based on the British show "Keep It in the Family:"

9 Spinoff of "Diff'rent Strokes" that originally featured Molly Ringwald

11 If the finale is to be believed, this 8-season show was all a dream of Robert Hartley

15 Howard Hesseman plays a history teacher to a class of gifted students

16 Yes, this popular *90s* show about nothing actually premiered in July of *1989.*

17 Spin off of "The Cosby Show", taking place at a historically black college in Virginia

18 Original name of "The Hogan Family;" it changed when the lead actress was fired

19 Harry Anderson comedy that took place mostly in a Manhattan Criminal Courthouse

20 Everyone knows this one's name

21 Show centering around the Seaver family, starring Alan Thicke and Joanna Kerns

22 Series with two men who are awarded joint custody of an orphaned girl *because they don't know which one's the baby daddy.*

DOWN

1 Robert Guillaume stars as a governor's head of household

3 Gordon Shumway, from planet Melmac, crash-lands on Earth. Hijinks ensue

4 Susan Saint James and Jane Curtain are two divorced women who move in together

5 Tony Danza is a live-in housekeeper. It is unclear who has control here.

6 Two men dress up as women so they can live in a female-only apartment building. Yes, it was a creepy concept then too.

8 Four retired women live together in a house in Miami.

10 Ricky Schroeder is a young boy sent to live with his wealthy playboy father

12 This Thursday night sitcom was the number one show in America for five seasons, tying a record that was set by "All in the Family."

13 Spin-off of a recurring series of sketches featured on "The Carol Burnett Show;" starred Vicki Lawrence

14 Sherman Hemsley plays an ambulance chasing lawyer who is also a deacon at his Philadelphia church

HORROR MOVIES 1

solution on page 105

ACROSS

3 Terry O'Quinn plays a serial killer who marries a widow with a suspicious teenage daughter

5 A stray cat links three stories, two of which are based on Stephen King story stories

7 This 1982 film by Tobe Hooper focuses on a suburban home plagued by malevolent ghosts

10 A horror author wants to write a book about Vietnam in the home he inherited, but he finds himself haunted by visions and monsters

13 Stephen King directed this film about electronic devices that turn on their users

14 Dee Wallace is a news anchor stalked by a serial killer. Thankfully the serial killer is killed. But then he's a werewolf. Yeah, it's a lot.

15 Farmer Vincent is famous for his fantastic smoked meats. Do I really have to tell you what the secret ingredient is?

16 A pair of intergalactic bounty hunters pursue a group of small, furry aliens called "Krites" that have landed in rural Kansas.

17 A young man in Oklahoma gets involved with a family of nomadic vampires in this neo-Western directed by Kathryn Bigelow

18 David Cronenberg's 1986 remake of the Vincent Price classic starred Jeff Goldblum and Geena Davis

19 Two boys release a horde of demons from a hole in their backyard.

DOWN

1 Three college kids attempt to hire a stripper for their party. They picked Grace Jones, who happens to be a vampire. Oops.

2 George Romero and Stephen King teamed up for this homage to EC Comics

4 A town reinstates their long-suspended Valentine's Day dance, incurring the wrath of a maniac in mining gear

5 A 1958 Plymouth Fury has a bad attitude

6 Two students steal a body from a cryogenics lab, not realizing its actually under the control of an alien slug. Hijinks ensue

8 Rutger Hauer terrorizes C. Thomas Howell across the highways of West Texas.

9 Wheelchair-bound Corey Haim suspects there's a werewolf in town. **Spoiler**: yup.

10 Clive Barker's classic about a mysterious puzzle box that summons extradimensional beings called Cenobites

11 Jeremy Irons plays twin gynecologists in this David Cronenberg psychological thriller

12 There's too many damn vampires in Santa Carla, California.

CARTOONS

solution on page 105

ACROSS

3 Lydia explores the Netherworld with the titular ghostly con man

5 Disney's first major serialized cartoon series, starred Gruffi, Zummi, Grammi, Tummi…

8 This series was adapted from the Japanese anime shows "Beast King GoLion" and the unrelated "Armored Fleet Dairugger XV"

10 In a post-apocalyptic wasteland, this title character traveled with Ariel and Ookla the Mok

14 One of the most successful Saturday morning cartoons ever, based on characters created by Pierre "Peyo" Culliford

15 A young girl named Wisp is given magical powers to spread color and beauty throughout the land.

17 Like 8-across, this series was adapted and used footage from 3 anime titles, including "Super Dimensional Fortress Macross"

18 It's all fun and games until Lion-O breaks out the Sword of Omens. Then it's ON.

19 Another Hasbro-inspired cartoon, this one taking place in the magical land of Ponyland.

20 Titular characters fight enemies like Shredder and Krang; mentored by Splinter.

DOWN

1 Flash Gordon, Mandrake the Magician, and The Phantom team up against Ming the Merciless and other assorted baddies..

2 The continuing adventures of Scrooge McDuck and his nephews

4 Don Adams voices this cyborg cop, but his niece and her dog actually do all the work…

6 Sci-Fi / Western series that takes place on New Texas

7 Before there was PAW Patrol, there were these dogs who had to outwit their human friend's evil guardian, Katrina Stoneheart

9 Title characters live in a place called the Kingdom of Caring Oh, and they're bears.

10 This cartoon was based on a very popular Hasbro toy line (that were themselves inspired by Japanese Diaclone toys)

11 Jim Henson's beloved characters presented as toddlers in a nursery

12 Military action-adventure show based on Hasbro's long dormant toy line

13 A rock singer inherits her father's holographic computer and it's all truly outrageous

16 Contemporary of He-Man, Adora was also known as the Princess of Power in this series

3 TV CHARACTERS IN SEARCH OF A SHOW

For this puzzle, I'm giving you three characters from a show.
Fill in the grid on page 25 with the name of the show.

ACROSS

3 Madolyn Hayes, David Addison, Jr., Agnes DiPesto

8 Chief William O. "Bill" Gillespie, Detective Virgil Tibbs, Officer V. L. "Bubba" Skinner

9 Miles Silverberg, Jim Dial, Corky Sherwood

10 Valerie Hogan, David Hogan, Willie Hogan

11 Governor Eugene X. Gatling, Gretchen Kraus, Benson DuBois

12 Kip / Buffy Wilson, Henry / Hildegard Desmond, Amy Cassidy

14 Blair, Natalie, Tootie

16 Ricky Stratton, Edward Statton III, Kate Summers Stratton

19 Jamie, Buddy, Charles

20 Jonathan Hart, Jennifer Hart, Max

24 Dan, Jackie, Darlene

26 Vinnie Terranova, Frank McPike, Daniel Burroughs (a.k.a. Lifeguard)

28 Dorothy, Rose, Blanche

30 Bobby, Sue Ellen, J. R.

31 Cathy Lee Crosby, John Davidson, Fran Tarkenton (wait, those are real people)

32 George Papaopoulos, Susan Clark, Webster Long

DOWN

1 Dr. Douglas Howser, Vinnie Salvatore Delpino, Mary Margaret Spaulding

2 Capt. Francis Xavier "Frank" Furillo, Joyce Davenport, Sgt Phil Freemason Esterhaus

4 Karen Fairgate MacKenzie, Valerie Ewing, Abby Fairgate

5 Cowboy Curtis, Jambi, Miss Yvonne

6 Robert McCall, Mickey Kostmayer, Control

7 Thelma, Vinton, Naomi

13 Julia, Suzanne, Charlene

14 Rick, Neil, Vyvyan

15 Kelly Kapowski, Zack Morris, Jessie Spano

17 Harry Stone, Christine Sullivan, Dan Fielding

18 Al, Peg, Bud

19 Sam, Diane, Norm

21 Willie Tanner, Lynn Tanner, Gordon Shumway

22 Denise Huxtable, Whitley Gilbert, Dwayne Wayne

23 Carl Winslow, Harriette Winslow, Steve Urkel

25 Deacon Ernest Frye, Thelma Frye, Reverend Reuben Gregory

27 Danny, Jesse, Joey

29 Dick Loudon, George Utley, Stephanie Vanderkellen

3 CHARACTERS IN SEARCH OF A SHOW

solution on page 105

AS FEATURED ON THE ORIGINAL MOTION PICTURE SOUNDTRACK

For this one, you'll need to identify the movie in which these songs were prominently featured.
An asterisk indicates that the song was not written *directly* for the film, but was still in it.

solution on page 105

ACROSS

2	I'm Alright
4	The Hero
6	Magic Dance
8	I Melt With You*
9	Who's Johnny
19	Meet Me Half Way
22	Cry Little Sister
23	Eye of the Tiger
24	I Just Called to Say I Love You
25	In Your Eyes*

DOWN

1	Holiday Road
3	Fight the Power
5	All Over the World
7	(I've Had) The Time of My Life
10	On the Road Again
11	Everybody Wants to Rule the World*
12	I Can Dream About You
13	Holding Out for a Hero
14	Take a Look at Me Now
15	Veteran of the Psychic Wars*
16	Like to Get to Know You Well*
17	Crazy for You
18	Cruel Summer*
20	If You Leave
21	Let the River Run

GENERAL KNOWLEDGE 5

solution on page 106

ACROSS

1 1980 comedy that is a parody of the disaster film genre, notably 1957s "Zero Hour!"

5 1980 comedy that reunited Gene Wilder and Richard Pryor, "_____ Crazy"

6 Cable channel that officially launched on August 1, 1981 with footage of the first space shuttle launch countdown

7 Music video combining live action with pencil-sketch animation was by this band

8 This Reginald VelJohnson sitcom was a spin-off of "Perfect Strangers."

11 Game 3 of the 1989 World Series was delayed by 10 days when the Loma Prieta _________ occurred

12 This absurdist comic by Gary Larson debuted on January 1, 1980

14 This former Beatle was murdered outside his New York apartment building in 1980.

15 Quirky 1989 crime film with Kevin Kline and Alan Rickman, "The ________ Man"

17 1986 Stallone film with a script based on revisions intended for "Beverly Hills Cop"

18 1981 black comedy; John Belushi's final film

DOWN

2 Dennis Quaid, Bill Murray, and Mel Gibson were all offered the lead in this film; it would go on to earn Dustin Hoffman an Oscar

3 The original location of this Shakespearean theater was lost until a foundation was discovered in 1989.

4 1980 hockey game between the US and the Soviet Union; called the "_____ on Ice"

6 Popular line of jackets in the 80s.

9 Operation El Dorado Canyon was a US air strike on terrorist centers in this country

10 British soap opera, set in fictional Walford, that premiered in 1985

13 What people called the aliens in "V"

16 The second best-selling record of the 80s (after Thriller) was by this rock band

SCI-FI MOVIES 1

solution on page 106

ACROSS

1 Title of Star Wars: Episode V

10 Slacker kid finds a strange orb that's a relic from a crashed UFO, decides to use it for his science class project. Hijinks ensue.

11 Immortals sword fight to kill each other. Yes, that sentence has a glaring contradiction, and it *still makes more sense than the sequels.*

12 Warwick Davis is a peck farmer who must protect a baby princess from an evil sorceress

14 Beloved 1987 Rob Reiner film; an adaptation of William Goldman's fantasy novel

17 A botanist misses his ride home, and someone at M&M got fired for saying "no" to that product placement deal.

18 A high school slacker-hacker thinks he's playing a computer game. The computer doesn't.

19 A robot is sent back in time to kill the mother of the leader of the future human resistance.

DOWN

1 A young boy joins a group of thieves who plunder treasure from different points in history.

2 A timid architect's new PC becomes sentient and falls in love.

3 A detective must hunt down and "retire" refugee robots in a futuristic Los Angeles

4 A military robot gains sentience after being struck by lightning; goes on the run

5 A plastic surgeon becomes embroiled in a mind-control plot using CG performers

6 A young girl offers her brother to the goblin king, then reneges on the deal.

7 Title of Star Wars: Episode VI

8 Homeless men discover sunglasses that allow the wearer to see the real world

9 Adult animated sci-fi fantasy anthology film that featured the voices of many SCTV alums, as well as a rockin' soundtrack

13 At night, he turns into a wolf. At dawn, she turns into a hawk Can these two crazy kids really keep their relationship together?

15 Emilio Estevez plays a young fella who gets a job with a car repossession agency and gets in over his head trying to find a certain car with something mysterious in the trunk

16 A prince and his companions set out to rescue his bride from the Beast and his army of alien soldiers.

MOVIE TAGLINES

Can you match the poster/video box tagline with the proper movie?

solution on page 106

ACROSS

2 They're here

4 They're here to save the world

7 He loved the American Dream. With a vengeance

9 Half man. Half Machine. All cop.

10 When he pours, he reigns

11 Where everything seems possible and nothing is what it seems.

13 They're on a mission from God.

14 The next great adventure.

17 It's 4am. Do you know where your car is?

19 You think they're people just like you. You're wrong. Dead wrong.

20 Deeds not words!

21 Everything you've heard is true

22 It's not just a game anymore

23 Every dream has a price

25 Talent made him a star. Fate made him a legend

27 Crime is a disease. Meet the cure.

28 Meet the guy who changes his identity more often than he changes his underwear

29 There can be only one.

30 This time, It's personal

31 Thank god it's only a motion picture!

DOWN

1 It is everything you've dreamed of. It is nothing you expect.

3 The dancing's over. Now it gets dirty.

5 A world inside a computer where man has never been. Until now.

6 Man has made his match. Now it's *his* problem.

8 A tale of murder, lust, greed, revenge, and seafood

12 40 stories of sheer adventure

15 Man is the warmest place to hide

16 Be afraid. Be very afraid.

18 The first casualty of war is innocence

24 This time it's war

26 Have you ever had a really big secret?

ONE HIT WONDERS 1

A one hit wonder is a band that only charted once. It doesn't mean they only had one good song, mind you, just that only one really broke through. How many of these do you remember, and who did them?

solution on page 106

ACROSS

1 Come on, Eileen
4 In a Big Country
6 Take on Me
9 I Know What Boys Like
12 88 Lines about 44 Women
13 Man in Motion (St. Elmo's Fire)
14 Oh Yeah.
17 I Ran
19 Our House
21 Whip It
22 Turning Japanese
23 Let the Music Play
24 Genius of Love
25 Two of Hearts
26 Too Shy
27 Mickey
28 You Spin Me Right Round (Like a Record)
29 I Melt With You

DOWN

2 Tainted Love
3 Catch Me (I'm Falling)
4 I Want Candy
5 Video Killed the Radio Star
7 99 Luftballoons
8 Mexican Radio
10 It's Raining Men
11 Harden my Heart
15 867-5309
16 Electric Avenue
18 Funkytown
20 Cars

GENERAL KNOWLEDGE 6

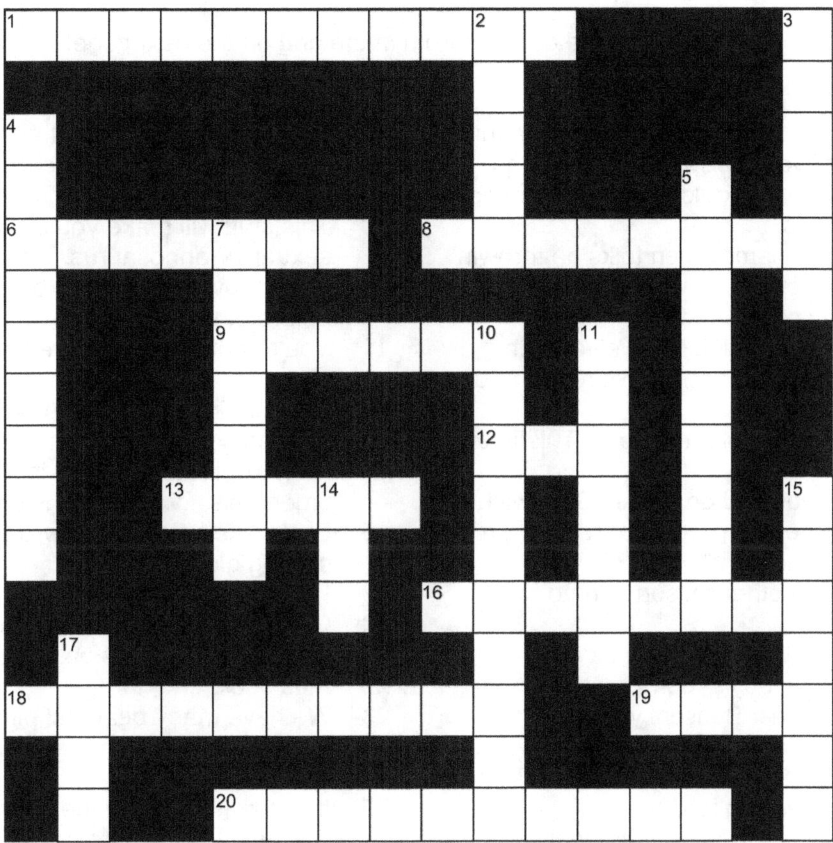

solution on page 106

ACROSS

1 The movie bombed big time, but this singer had a massive hit with the soundtrack to the movie "The Jazz Singer"

6 Multi-venue concert held on July 13, 1985, to raise funds for famine relief

8 "A Christmas Story" was based on the writings of author Jean ________

9 Recipient of the first ever Makeup Oscar, "An American Werewolf in ______"

12 News network launched on June 1, 1980

13 Genesis' bestselling album, "Invisible ____"

16 Nickname for Margaret Thatcher. *Be nice.*

18 British band that had a #1 hit with a remake of Shocking Blue's 1969 song "Venus"

19 Mary McDonnell's role in "Dances with Wolves," Stands with a ____

20 Invented in 1976 and released internationally in 1980, this combination puzzle is the world's bestselling puzzle game, having sold over 450 million units.

DOWN

2 Directorial debut of the author of "The Exorcist," 1980's "The ____ Configuration"

3 This 1980 musical fantasy features Gene Kelly in his final film role.

4 NY hockey team that won the Stanley Cup four years in a row

5 Tragedy struck this band in 1986, when their bassist was killed in a bus accident

7 Ally Sheedy's character in "The Breakfast Club," the basket case

10 Cheech and Chong's third film, in which they sell cannabis out of an ice cream truck

11 San Francisco won four Super Bowls with him as their quarterback, Joe ________

14 Music station that debuted on March 5, 1983, beating competitor The Nashville Network by two days

15 1982 fantasy film co-directed by Jim Henson and Frank Oz, "The Dark _______"

17 Member of Hans Gruber's "Die Hard" team that was played by Alexander Godunov

MOVIES QUOTES 1

Put the movie the quote is from in the grid on the next page!

ACROSS

3 Went away? "I dwell in darkness without you" and it *"went away?"*

9 Chew, if only you could see what I've seen with your eyes.

14 That's a real shame when folks be throwin' away a perfectly good white boy like that.

16 They mostly come at night. Mostly.

17 We're American soldiers! We've been kicking ass for 200 years! We're ten and one!

18 We're not really violent people. This is our first gun.

21 The review you had on "Shark Sandwich," which was merely a two word review, just said "Shit Sandwich."

24 Now I have another reason to hate Christmas.

27 What's this? We don't have a candy machine in the boy's room!

30 Oh, Benson. Dear Benson, you are so mercifully free of the ravages of intelligence.

31 Can we keep this…between us? I'd hate to lose my teaching job.

32 Haven't you ever heard of the healing power of laughter?

34 Suck my fat one, you cheap dimestore hood.

37 Go ahead. Make my day.

38 When you stop to smell the flowers, are they afraid?

39 He's a sailor, he's in New York; we get this guy laid, we won't have any trouble!

40 Listen, we're not just doing this for money. We're doing it for a shitload of money!

41 I've been dating too. Nice girl. An author. She wrote the book on male sexual dysfunction. You've probably read it.

42 You better get yourself a garlic t-shirt, buddy, or it's your funeral!

DOWN

1 People on ludes should not drive.

2 Come on over here, sugarbuns! This machine just called me an asshole!

4 What kind of asshole grows up in Seattle and doesn't even know how to swim?

5 Welcome to the party, pal!

6 I know you are but what am I?

7 Man who catch fly with chopstick, accomplish anything.

8 This stuff will make you a goddamned sexual Tyrannosaurus, just like me.

10 Hey, baby, you must've been something before electricity!

11 You're not too smart, are you? I like that in a man.

12 Life is pain, highness. Anyone who says differently is selling something.

13 All of my filth is arranged in alphabetical order. This, for instance, is under "H" for toy.

15 Looks like I picked the wrong week to quit sniffing glue

19 I hate Illinois Nazis.

20 Give me the justice department. Entertainment Division.

22 Kids suck.

23 We have many beautiful pinatas for your birthday celebration, each one filled with little surprises!

25 It occurs to me that the best way to hurt rich people is by turning them into poor people.

26 Did you mom marry Mr. Rogers?

28 I tied my own shoes once. It is an overrated experience.

29 Will you hold my wallet for me while I take this test, please? There's a thousand dollars in there…or maybe there isn't.

33 Frankly, Scarlet, I don't give a damn.

35 Pretty soon, a woobie isn't enough. You're out on the street trying to score an electric blanket, or maybe a quilt. And the next thing you know, you're strung out on bedspreads Ken. That's serious.

36 I'm not the first guy who fell in love with a woman that he met in a restaurant who turned out to be the daughter of a kidnapped scientist, only to lose her to her childhood lover who she last saw on a deserted island, who then turned out fifteen years later to be the leader of the French underground…

MOVIES QUOTES 1

solution on page 107

BOOKS

For this puzzle, you must identfy the author of the well known book (surnames only).

solution on page 107

ACROSS

2 The Handmaid's Tale
6 Ender's Game
9 The Satanic Verses
10 Battlefield Earth
14 The Color Purple
15 The Remains of the Day
17 The Gunslinger
19 White Noise
21 Ancient Evenings
22 Watchers
24 Contact
26 Lake Wobegone Days
27 The Prince of Tides
28 The Hunt for Red October
29 Love in the Time of Cholera
31 The Pillars of the Earth
32 The Bonfire of the Vanities
33 The Joy Luck Club
34 Lonesome Dove

DOWN

1 North and South
2 The Restaurant at the End of the Universe
3 The B.F.G.
4 Ham on Rye
5 Discworld
7 The Little Drummer Girl
8 Beloved
10 Red Dragon
11 Perfume
12 A Brief History of Time
13 A Confederacy of Dunces
15 The Cider House Rules
16 The Hellbound Heart
18 Neuromancer
20 The Bourne Identity
23 The Vampire Lestat
25 Blood Meridian
26 The Unbearable Lightness of Being
30 The Name of the Rose

GENERAL KNOWLEDGE 7

solution on page 108

ACROSS

3 1980 Eastwood flick "______ Billy"

4 English pop band that hit the US Top 20 with "You Spin Me Round (Like a Record)"

8 1981 Lily Tomlin / Charles Grodin film "The Incredible ______ Woman"

9 This fruit was marketed in the mid-80s with commercials featuring a fictional R&B band rendered in Claymation.

10 Food choice that Vern in "Stand By Me" would happily eat for the rest of his life.

12 Her single "Let the Music Play" is thought by some to be the start of the "dance pop" era

13 Last of the original Love Bug films, released in 1980; "Herbie Goes ________"

15 Her first screen appearance was opposite Jeff Goldblum in 1989's "The Tall Guy"

17 Alison Dooley's character in "Indiana Jones and the Last Crusade"

19 Band formed by surviving members of Joy Division after Ian Curtis' death

20 He played Killian in "The Running Man"

DOWN

1 Graceland opened to the public in 1982 in this city

2 Utterly bizarre 1981 comedy that features jeans with ripped out backsides (and exposed buttocks) as a new fashion trend.

3 VHS defeated this format to win the videotape format war of the 1980s.

5 Gorbachev's political slogan (used together with perestroika)

6 "Ice cream of the future," invented in 1988

7 Nancy Reagan's anti-drug slogan

11 1980 Bette Midler film, "Divine ______"

12 1981 Cronenberg film, infamous for an early scene with a exploding head

14 Sandra Day ________, first woman to serve on the United States Supreme Court

16 New Wave band that famously wore "Energy Dome" hats (often mistaken for flowerpots)

18 English rock band that scored their biggest US hit with 1989's "Mayor of Simpleton"

EMMY AWARDS

ACROSS

2 This police procedural won Best Drama four years straight (1981-1984)
5 This Harry Hamlin-led legal show won Best Drama in 1987
7 He won lead actor in a comedy for playing Alex Reiger in "Taxi" in 1981 and 1983
9 Michael J. Fox won lead actor in a comedy three years straight for this show
11 This show, set in a police station, won best comedy for its final season in 1982
12 Tom Selleck won Best Actor in a Drama in 1984 for this show
16 One of the leads in 35-across, she won Best Actress in a Drama in 1986 and 1987
18 John Hillerman won Best Supporting Actor in 1987 for this role in "Magnum PI"
19 Nominated four times, he won Best Supporting in 1981 for playing Louie De Palma on "Taxi"
22 Winner of Best Comedy Series in 1986 and 1987; also notable because all four of the female leads won for their performances (not all at the same time, of course)
25 Winner of 1988's Best Drama, this show was influenced by movies like "The Big Chill" in how it presented the lives of a group of Philadelphia baby boomers
26 Won Supporting Actress in comedy in 1982 and 1983 for playing Simka Dahblitz-Gravas on "Taxi"
27 Won Best Actress in 1988 for playing Dorothy on the show in 22-across
28 Harry Morgan and Loretta Swit both won Supporting awards in 1980 for this show
31 Robert Guillaume won 1985's Best Actor in a comedy for his titular role in this show
33 Won Best Actress in 1987 for playing Blanche on the show in 22-across
34 In 1981, Isabel Sanford became the first (and, to date, *only*) African American woman to win Lead Actress in a Comedy for this show
35 This female-driven police procedural won Best Drama in 1985 and 1986, while its two lead actresses won Best Actress in a Drama every year from 1983 to1988
36 Powers Booth won Lead in a Special for his performance as this cult leader in "Guyana Tragedy"
38 Boston bar-set show that won Best Comedy Series in 1983 and 1984
39 One of the leads 35-across, she won Best Actress in a Drama for 1983, 1984, 1985, and 1988
41 Cathryn Damon and Richard Mulligan won both Comedy Leads in 1980 for this show
42 This coming-of-age show won Best Comedy in 1988, *after only six episodes had aired*

DOWN

1 Rhea Perlman won Supporting Actress from 1984 through 1986 for playing this role on 38-across
3 Pat Harrington, Jr. won Supporting Actor in 1984 for playing this "One Day at a Time" character
4 Ensemble comedy led by Judd Hirsch that won Best Comedy in 1980 and 1981
6 Won Best Actress in a Comedy for her role as Diane Chambers in 38-across
7 Christoper Lloyd won Supporting Actor in a Comedy in 1982 and 1983 for playing the "Taxi" character Reverend ___ Ignatowski
8 Historical drama about feudal Japan, won Best Limited Series in 1981
10 Winner of Best Drama in 1980, this show was the third spin-off of "The Mary Tyler Moore Show"
13 Versatile actor who won 1986's Lead Actor in a Special for "Death of a Salesman"
14 He won Best Actor in 1984 for the final season of "Three's Company"
15 Eileen Brennan won Supporting Actress in a comedy for reprising her film role in this 1981 show
17 Bruce Willis won Best Actor in a Drama in 1987 for this show
20 She won Best Actress in 1986 for playing Rose on the show in 22-across
21 In 1982, this actor won his sixth Lead Actor Emmy for playing Hawkeye on "MASH"
23 Won Best Supporting actress in 1988 for playing Sophia on the show in 22-across
24 This SNL alum won Best Actress in a Comedy in 1984 and 1985 for "Kate and Allie"
29 She won 1980's Best Actress in a Special for playing Anne Sullivan in "The Miracle Worker," 18 years after winning an Academy Award for playing Helen Keller
30 This very popular show about the Huxtable family won Best Comedy Series in 1985.

32 This medical drama earned acting awards like crazy! Ed Flanders, James Coco, and Doris Roberts each won once, while William Daniels and Bonnie Bartlett won twice

37 He won Best Lead in a *Drama* in 1980 for the same role that earned him three Emmy Awards in the seventies for Supporing Role in a *Comedy*. Pretty good trick, huh?

40 While this show ran for 14 seasons and 357 episodes, the only *major* Emmy it won was for Lead Actress in a Drama in 1980 (won by Barbara Bel Geddes)

solution on page 107

FILM DEBUTS

A lot of big names had their film debuts in the 80s. How many of these first films can you remember?

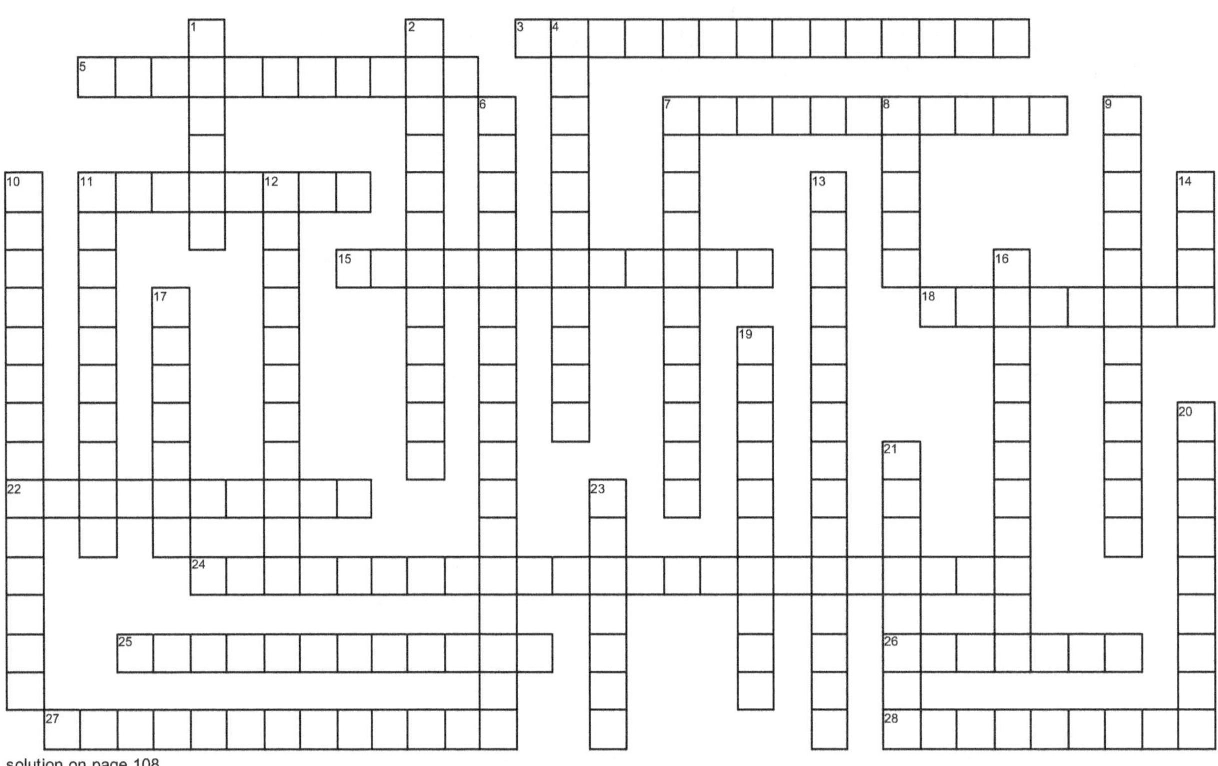

solution on page 108

ACROSS

3 Christian Bale
5 Rene Russo
7 Bruce Campbell
11 Kathleen Turner
15 Benicio Del Toro
18 Woody Harrelson *and* Wesley Snipes
22 Fairuza Balk
24 Glen Close
25 Julia Roberts
26 Chris Cooper
27 Kevin Kline
28 Jerry O'Connell

DOWN

1 Robin Williams
2 Brad Pitt
4 Matt Damon

6 Tom Hanks
7 Jason Bateman
8 Winona Ryder
9 Richard E. Grant
10 Adam Sandler
11 Nicole Kidman
12 Tom Cruise
13 Matthew Broderick
14 Sean Penn
16 Frances McDormand
17 Alan Rickman
19 Josh Brolin
20 Bruce Willis
21 Michael Madsen
23 Geena Davis

GENERAL KNOWLEDGE 8

solution on page 108

ACROSS

3 1987 Sylvester Stallone arm-wrestling epic.
4 Unofficial sequel to "The Rocky Horror Picture Show"
7 This boxer won 15 fights in 1985, eventually clinching the heavyweight title in 1986.
10 This band composed the majority of the score for 1984's "Dune"
12 In 1987, Reagan demanded the razing of the Berlin Wall at the Brandenberg ____
13 Baby's actual first name in "Dirty Dancing"
14 TV show prominently sampled in the 1988 song "What's on Your Mind (Pure Energy)"
17 Host city of the 1988 Summer Olympics
18 On September 1, 1985, the research vessel Knorr found the wreckage of this ship
19 1980 musical film; inspired a 1982 TV series

DOWN

1 1981 Stephen King novel, adapted into a 1983 film with Dee Wallace
2 Dance move debuted by Michael Jackson on the 1983 TV Special "Motown 25"
4 Washington stratovolcano that erupted on May 18, 1980, Mount ____ ____
5 Spike Lee's "She's Gotta Have It" character, appeared in many Nike ads
6 Because the source material was a sequel, producers of "Die Hard" were contractually obligated to offer the film to this 73 year old actor / crooner before hiring Bruce Willis
8 Often called "rooster sauce" or "cock sauce," this hot sauce was introduced to the US in the 1980s by Huy Fong Foods.
9 Agent Maxwell Smart from "Get Smart" returned in 1980's "The ____ Bomb"
11 Anthony Michael Hall's character in "Sixteen Candles" was called Farmer ___
15 An Asian immigrant unknowingly gets involved in a cocaine smuggling operation in the 1982 comedy "They Call Me ____"
16 A 1980 remake of the Swedish film "Intermezzo," Willie Nelson starred in "Honeysuckle ____"

ACADEMY AWARDS WINNERS

ACROSS

3 1988's Best Picture about brothers on an unexpected road trip (in-between showings of Wapner)

5 1984's Best Picture, a fictionalized story of the rivalry between two composers based on a play

6 Best Actor of 1985 for "Kiss of the Spider Woman"

12 Won Best Actress of 1980 for playing Loretta Lynn in "Coal Miner's Daughter"

18 This English actor won Best Actor in 1989 for his work in "My Left Foot"

19 She won 1987's Best Actress for "Moonstruck"

22 This 1987 film won all nine award it was nominated for, including Best Picture, Adapted Screenplay, Art Direction, Editing, Score and Best Director for Bernardo Bertolucci

25 This 1986 film, based on the director's experience in Vietnam, won Best Picture

30 This 1982 biopic snagged awards for Best Picture, Director, Actor, and five others

31 She won Best Actress in 1985 for "The Trip to Bountiful"

32 This actress was only 21 when she won Best Actress for 1986's "Children of a Lesser God," making her the youngest winner in that category as well as the first dead winner in Oscar history

35 Won Best Director twice in the 80s – one for 25-across and one for "Born on the Fourth of July"

38 1981's Best Picture, chronicling two British athletes in the 1924 Olympics

39 1982's Best Supporting Actress for "Tootsie," the only Oscar the movie won (nominated for ten!)

40 Winner of 1988's Supporting Actress Award for her role as an eccentric dog trainer in "The Accidental Tourist"

41 Born Krishna Pandit Bhanji, this English actor won Best Actor in 1982 for the title role in "Gandhi"

42 This actor won 1985's Supporting Actor for his role in "Cocoon"

43 Twenty-five years after "The Hustler," he earned his first Academy Award for Best Actor for reprising his role of Fast Eddie Felson in 1986's "The Color of Money"

44 1989's Best Supporting Actor went to him for playing Sergeant Major John Rawlins in "Glory"

DOWN

1 1988's Best Director winner, for 3-across

2 The Academy must have liked – no, *really liked* her performance in 1984's "Places in the Heart," since they awarded her Best Actress

4 This British actor was famously unable to accept his 1986 Supporting Actor award for "Hannah and Her Sisters" because he was stuck on the set of "Jaws: The Revenge"

7 Best Director winner for 30-across

8 She won 1983's Best Actress award for her role as Aurora Greenfield in "Terms of Endearment"

9 This actress won her fourth Best Actress Award in 1981 for "On Golden Pond,"

10 She won 1982's Best Supporting Actress for playing a man in "The Year of Living Dangerously"

11 Winner of 1980's Best Picture, this film follows the tribulations of a family following a son's death

13 Morgan Freeman reprised his role from Off-Broadway in this film, 1989's winner for Best Picture

14 Best Actor winner for 3-across.

15 He won 1987's Best Actor for his performance as corporate raider Gordon Gekko in "Wall Street:

16 Already a TV heavyweight for co-creating "Rhoda," "Lou Grant," and "Taxi,: he won Best Director in 1983 for "Terms of Endearment"

17 Best Director winner for 5-across

20 This star of 1981's "Reds" won Best Director for his work behind the camera

21 This English actor won 1981's Supporting Actor award for his work as Hobson in "Arthur"

23 Director of 35-down

24 Winner of Best Actor for 1983's "Tender Mercies"

26 Won Best Actor for his work opposite 9-down in "On Golden Pond"

27 Best Director for 11-down

28 1988's Supporting Actor winner for his role as the oafish Otto in "A Fish Called Wanda"

29 1989's winner for "Driving Miss Daisy," she is still the oldest winner (at 80) for Best Actress

32 Nominated 6 times in the 1980s, this actress won Best Actress for 1982's "Sophie's Choice"

33 1987's Supporting Actor recipient for playing Malone in "The Untouchables"
35 1985 drama with Robert Redford and Meryl Streep; won Best Picture
36 1988 Best Actress for her performance in "The Accused"
37 1980 Best Actor winner for portraying boxer Jake LaMotta in "Raging Bull"

solution on page 109

BOTH KINDS OF MUSIC – COUNTRY *AND* WESTERN

Can you identify the singers of these 1980's country/western hits?

solution on page 108

ACROSS

1 Paradise Tonight
3 I Love a Rainy Night
6 Mountain Music
7 Always on My Mind
9 A Better Man
11 Let's Chase Each Other Around the Room
13 I'm Only in it for the Love
14 Lost in the Fifties Tonight
18 Fire and Smoke
20 Fool Hearted Memory
21 Why Not Me
22 It Ain't Easy Bein' Easy
23 Scarlet Fever
24 I Was Country When Country Wasn't Cool
25 I Believe in You
26 Don't Cheat in Our Hometown
27 Good Ol' Boys (Dukes of Hazzard)

DOWN

2 The Sound of Goodbye
4 Three Time Loser
5 I'll Never Stop Loving You
8 Red Neckin' Love Makin' Night
10 I Always Get Lucky with You
12 9 to 5
15 Wild and Blue
16 God Bless the U.S.A.
17 On the Other Hand
19 Night Games

GENERAL KNOWLEDGE 9

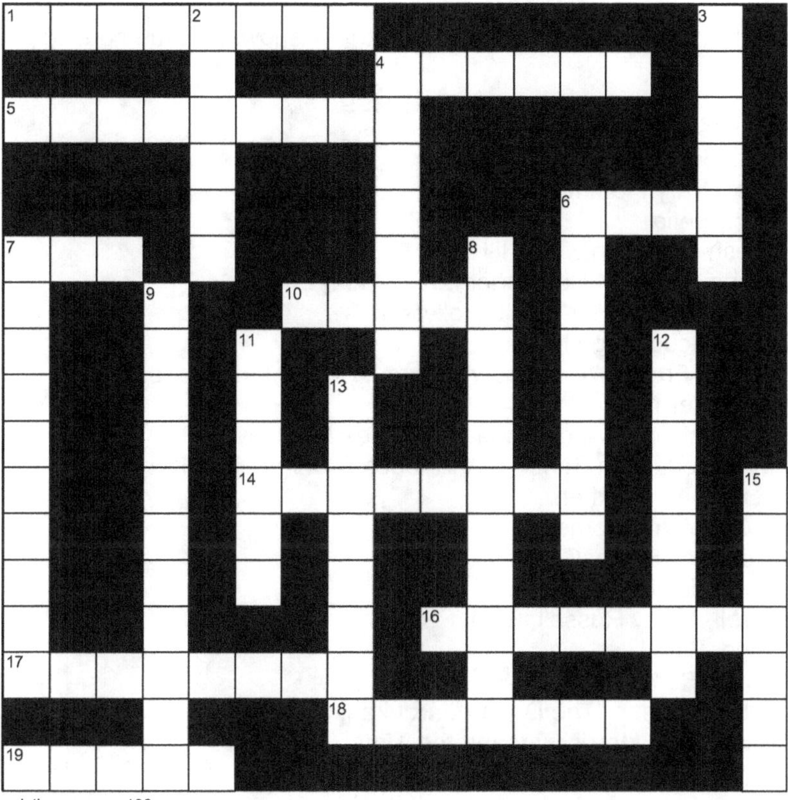

solution on page 108

ACROSS

1 1983 Dudley Moore film that inexplicably features Sir Alec Guinness as the ghost of Sigmund Freud. Yeah, really.

4 The iconic "Blown Away" ad campaign promoted this brand of hi-fi cassette

5 This 1986 Disney TV movie features a family that moves to Lucifer Falls, NH. You can already see a problem, right?

6 From 1981's "Mommie Dearest:" "No _____ hangers EVER."

7 A-Team actor, real name Laurence Tureaud

10 1981 film, regarded by Roger Ebert as being the one film completely devoid of any cliches, "My Dinner with _____."

14 Morgan Freeman played high school principal Joe Clark in this 1989 film

16 Nike ad campaign, launched in 1988, that was inspired by an execution. No, really.

17 1985 sequel, "National Lampoon's _________ Vacation"

18 Primary villain of "Three Amigos"

19 Character in "The Terminator" sent back in time to protect Sarah Connor, Kyle _____.

DOWN

2 Underwater cartoon characters that *you know damn well* were a Smurfs rip-off

3 1980 body-horror film "Altered _____"

4 1985 doll intended for boys; partially inspired Chucky from "Child's Play"

6 Alan Moore's 1986/87 comic series that was a deconstruction of superheroes

7 This R&B singer bought his dad a handgun for Christmas; maybe should have just gotten him a sweater instead.

8 South African archbishop who was awarded the Nobel Prize in 1984

9 This comedy was a spin-off of "The Tracey Ullman Show"

11 Indiana Jones' competitor and primary antagonist of "Raiders of the Lost Ark"

12 This band was lovin' every minute of "Working for the Weekend"

13 Surname of the thespian who played the character "Tango" in "Tango and Cash"

15 1981 historical drama that featured the final film appearances of James Cagney and Pat O'Brien

THREE CHARACTERS IN A MOVIE

Okay, we did this a while back with TV shows. Same concept!

ACROSS

3	Daniel LaRusso, Johnny Lawrence, Ali Mills
5	R.J. MacReady, Childs, Dr. Blair
7	Nick Rivers, Hilary Flammond, Déjà vu
9	Celie, Albert, Sofia
13	Herbert West, Dan Cain, Carl Hill
16	Mookie, Buggin' Out, Mister Señor Love Daddy
18	Chris Knight, Mitch Taylor, Lazlo Hollyfeld
21	Westley, Buttercup, Inigo Montoya
22	Freddy Shoop, Francis "Chainsaw" Gremp, Anna-Maria Mazarelli
23	Kevin, Fidgit, Vermin
25	Detective Mike Norris, Andy Barclay, Charles Lee Ray
27	Connor MacLeod, Juan Sanchez-Villalobos Ramirez, The Kurgan
29	Heather, Heather, Heather
31	Dorothy, Mombi, the Nome King
32	Lane Meyer, Roy Stalin, Charles De Mar
34	Snake Pliskin, Brain, The Duke of New York
37	Miles Russell, Maizy Russell, Buck Russell
38	Dutch, Dillon, Billy
40	Akeem Joffer, Randy Watson, Saul
41	Jack Walsh, Jonathan "The Duke" Mardukas, Special Agent Alonzo Mosely
42	The Kid, Apollonia, Morris Day and the Time

DOWN

1	Ted Striker, Elaine Dickinson, Jive Lady
2	Jack Burton, Gracie Law, Egg Shen
4	Frederick Treves, John Merrick, Madge Kendal
5	Frank Drebin, Jane Spencer, Det. Nordberg
6	Hans Zarkov, Princess Aura, General Klytus
8	Max Renn, Nicki Brand, Dr. Brian O'Blivion
10	Ty Webb, Al Czervik, Judge Smails
11	Ripley, Hudson, Hicks
12	Rick Deckard, Roy Batty, Rachael
14	Bob McKenzie, Doug McKenzie, Brewmeister Smith
15	Bastian, Atreyu, Rockbiter
17	Charley Brewster, Peter Vincent, Jerry Dandrige
19	Sarah Connor, Kyle Reese, Dr. Silberman
20	Jack Crawford, Will Graham, Hannibal Lecter
24	John Dalton, Wade Garrett, Brad Wesley
26	Lone Star, Dark Helmet, Barf
28	Sean Crenshaw, Count Dracula, Frankenstein's Monster
30	Chandler Jarrell, Nee Nang, Sardo Numspa
33	Ben Richards, Damon Killian, Sub-Zero
35	Colonel John Matrix, Bennett, Sully
36	Kara Zor-El, Selena, Zaltar
39	Madmartigan, Sorsha, Queen Bavmorda

THREE CHARACTERS IN A MOVIE

Use the clues from the previous page for this grid.

solution on page 109

MADE IN THE '80s

Can you identify these celebrities who were born in the 1980s?

solution on page 109

ACROSS

1 Pop artist, a.k.a. "Mister Worldwide"
3 Actress who won 2017's Best Actress Oscar for her performance in "La-La Land"
5 Born in 1989, just like the name of her album
10 Singer/actress; broke through with singles "Just Dance" and "Poker Face"
11 Actor who gained worldwide recognition when he played Kylo Ren in the Star Wars sequels
13 Actor who has appeared as four different comic characters, most notably Captain America.
17 British actress best known for playing Daenerys Targaryen, the Mother of Dragons
18 Canadian actor, known for playing awkward characters in Superbad, Arrested Development
21 British singer who released the best-selling album of the 21st century, appropriately titled "21." Oh, and she was 21 when she did it.
22 Born Nora Lum (from Queens), this comedian made waves with 2012's song "My Vag."
23 Scottish actress known for playing Amy Pond in "Doctor Who" and Nebula in Marvel films

DOWN

2 Her "…Baby One More Time" album is the biggest selling album ever by a teenager
3 French actress who appeared as Vesper Lynd in "Casino Royale"
4 He created "In the Heights" and "Hamilton"
6 Canadian actor who achieved stardom with "The Notebook"
7 Won the Oscar for her performance in "Dreamgirls," which makes up for getting booted off "American Idol" 2 years earlier
8 Israeli-born actress who played Queen Amidala in the Star Wars prequels
9 Achieved early fame as "Veronica Mars"
12 Played Kirk in the Star Trek reboot
14 Actor who broke out with "Even Stevens"
15 She won a Best Actress Oscar for "Room"
16 Australian actress, best known for playing Shiv Roy on "Succession"
19 Swedish DJ who topped most European music charts with 2013's "Wake Me Up"
20 Canadian rapper who released international hit singles "Hotline Bling" and "One Dance"

GENERAL KNOWLEDGE 10

solution on page 109

ACROSS

1 1984 Jeff Bridges film that was a remake of 1947's "Out of the Past"

4 Intended to complement HBO, this cable network launched August 1, 1980.

7 At 84 years old, he had a Top 20 Country Music Hit with "I Wish I Was Eighteen Again"

9 1982 British musical film, based on the 1979 album by Pink Floyd

11 Statue broken by Chunk in "The Goonies"

14 Toy store in which the piano scene happens in "Big"

18 1980s ad campaign for Domino's Pizza, "Avoid the _____"

19 1980 mystery film with Angela Lansbury as Miss Marple, "The _____ Crack'd"

DOWN

2 First drink ordered by Marty McFly in "Back to the Future," not realizing that it hadn't been invented yet.

3 TBS gameshow where contestants competed at playing video games

4 Molly Ringwald's "Breakfast Club" character, the "princess"

5 1984's "The Adventures of Buckaroo Banzai Across the _____ Dimension"

6 1987 beloved Lucasfilm Games' graphic adventure video game, "_____ Mansion"

8 Introduced in 1982, this "Bloom County" character was a parody of "Garfield"

10 1981 medieval fantasy film featuring early appearances by Patrick Stewart, Liam Neeson, and Gabriel Byrne

12 1980 teen comedy with Tatum O'Neal and Kristy McNichol, "Little _____"

13 The one food Dr. Hathaway cannot stand in "Real Genius." *Never tell your enemy your weakness!*

15 Pizza restaurant founded in 1980, home to the Rock-a-fire Explosion.

16 Ben Edlund-created superhero parody, originally used as a mascot for New England Comics. Spoon!

17 First album to sell over one million compact discs, Dire Strait's "Brothers in _____"

THREE MOVIES, SAME ACTOR

We've done three actors in the same movie – now how about *one* actor in *three* movies?

ACROSS

1 Spies Like Us, Trading Places, Doctor Detroit
5 Frantic, Witness, The Mosquito Coast
15 The Man with Two Brains, Dirty Rotten Scoundrels, All of Me
16 Urban Cowboy, Legal Eagles, Black Widow
18 About Last Night, Wisdom, The Seventh Sign
19 Kiss of the Spider Woman, The Big Chill, Body Heat
20 The 'Burbs, The Man with One Red Shoe, The Empire Strikes Back
25 Fast Times at Ridgemont High, Ruthless People, Beverly Hills Cop
31 Bad Boys, At Close Range, Colors
33 Nighthawks, Tango and Cash, Lock Up
36 Police Story, The Protector. The Big Brawl
37 Tootsie, Beetlejuice, Transylvania 6-5000
38 Blue Velvet, Hoosiers, The Texas Chainsaw Massacre, Part 2
39 Stakeout, Tin Men, Down and Out in Beverly Hills
40 Harry and the Hendersons, Footloose, 2010: The Year We Make Contact
41 Biloxi Blues, Heaven's Gate, A View to a Kill
42 The Cotton Club, Quicksilver, A Nightmare on Elm Street 3: Dream Warriors

DOWN

2 River's Edge, Dangerous Liaisons, Bill and Ted's Excellent Adventure
3 Blind Date, Nadine, My Stepmother is an Alien
4 The Thing, Cocoon, Remo Williams: The Adventure Begins
6 Gung Ho, The Squeeze, Johnny Dangerously
7 The Year of Living Dangerously, Gorillas in the Mist, Aliens
8 Stir Crazy, Hanky Panky, See No Evil, Hear No Evil
9 Creepshow, The Right Stuff, The Abyss
10 Platoon, Major Leage, Rustlers' Rhapsody
11 Harlem Nights, 48 Hours, Beverly Hills Cop
12 The Presidio, Highlander, The Name of the Rose
13 Places in the Heart, Absence of Malice, Murphy's Romance
14 Little Shop of Horrors, Strange Brew, Ghostbusters
17 Sophie's Choice, A Fish Called Wanda, Silverado
21 Midnight Run, Angel Heart, The King of Comedy
22 Brewster's Millions, Harlem Nights, Jojo Dancer, Your Life is Calling
23 Jumpin' Jack Flash, The Color Purple, Burglar
24 Time Bandits, Silverado, Monty Python's Meaning of Life
25 The Killing Fields, Empire of the Sun, Dangerous Liaisons
26 Blade Runner, Splash, Wall Street
27 Romancing the Stone, Twins, Ruthless People
28 Angel Heart, Year of the Dragon, 9 ½ Weeks
29 Tequila Sunrise, Overboard, The Best of Times
30 Stripes. Scrooged, The Razor's Edge
31 Coal Miner's Daughter, Missing, The River
32 Lean on Me, Glory, Driving Miss Daisy
34 The Jewel of the Nile, Peggy Sue Got Married, Who Framed Roger Rabbit?
35 The Witches of Eastwick, Prizzi's Honor, The Shining
36 Tron, Jagged Edge, Tucker: The Man and His Dream

THREE MOVIES, SAME ACTOR

Use the clues on the left to fill in this grid.

GENERAL KNOWLEDGE 11

solution on page 110

ACROSS

1 This video rental store chain was founded by David Cook in 1985

4 The destination in 1983's "Vacation" was southern California's _____ World

6 Their album "Metal Health" was the first heavy metal album to top Billboard's album chart

7 She hosted Fox's first late night talk show, and *Johnny Carson never spoke to her again*

9 This 1981 board game was invented when its creators realized they were missing pieces of their Scrabble game.

14 This magical five-pointed throwing star was necessary to defeat the Beast in "Krull"

16 1980 slasher movie with Jamie Lee Curtis, "Terror _____"

17 Ricardo Montalban's Star Trek 2 role

18 Created in 1980, this zombie-like character is the mascot for Iron Maiden

19 This Chicago Bears running back was nicknamed "Sweetness"

DOWN

1 This artist, part of the Neo-expressionism movement, died in 1988 at the age of 27 from a heroin overdose.

2 This 1985 movie was released in theaters with three separate endings

3 This band was formed in Athens, Georgia in 1980 by University of Georgia students

5 Guns n' Roses' 1988 second album, which yielded only one single ("Patience")

8 Tom Hulce played the title character in this 1984 film, based on Peter Shaffer's play

10 Another 1980 slasher movie with Jamie Lee Curtis; this one also featured Leslie Nielsen.

11 1980's detective show in which two war vets operate the Pier 56 Detective Agency

12 In "Ghostbusters," this snack food is utilized to illustrate the amount of paranormal activity in New York City. *It would be a big one.*

13 Lipps Inc, a disco and funk group from Minneapolis, is best known for this single

15 1981 film in which Dudley Moore plays an alcoholic New York City millionaire

SEÑOR SPIELBERGO!

solution on page 110

ACROSS

3 He produced this hit 1988 Robert Zemeckis film about cartoon characters in Hollywood

5 He directed one shot in this 1983 Al Pacino gangster film.

7 He directed this 1987 coming-of-age war film based on J.G. Ballard's autobiographical novel

9 He produced this 1985 film, featuring the first starring role of Kevin Costner

13 He appeared as a Cook County Tax Assessor in this 1980 comedy

14 He directed this 1989 remake of "A Guy Named Joe"

15 He directed the "Kick the Can" segment of a movie based on this television show

17 He produced this 1988 animated feature about an orphaned dinosaur

19 He was co-executive producer of this 1986 Tom Hanks – Shelley Long film

20 He produced this 1982 Tobe Hooper movie. How involved was he? *That's up for debate.*

21 He wrote the story and produced this 1985 film, about kids looking for One-Eyed Willy

22 He directed this 1982 film, which was the top grossing film of all time (until his 1993 film)

DOWN

1 He was executive producer on this film, based on Sir Arthur Conan Doyle's works

2 He directed this 1989 sequel to 4-down, "Indiana Jones and the _____________"

4 He teamed up with George Lucas in 1981 to make this action-adventure film,

6 He executive produced this animated film about a mouse immigrating to America

8 He directed this 1984 prequel to 4-down, "Indiana Jones and the _____________"

10 He executive produced this 1985 time travel classic (and its sequels)

11 He executive produced this 1987 film about a miniaturized test pilot

12 He created this anthology TV series that ran for two seasons on NBC

13 He directed this 1985 adaptation of Alice Walker's Pulitzer Prize winning novel

16 He executive produced this 1980 black comedy starring Kurt Russell as a devious automobile salesman

18 He executive produced this classic 1984 film, about *mogwai* which (along with 8-down) led to the creation of the PG-13 rating

TOP 1980s ALBUMS

You've been provided the names of the albums. Who's the artist?

solution on page 110

ACROSS

3	Hanging Tough
4	Faith
6	Purple Rain
8	Appetite for Destruction
10	Born in the USA
12	No Jacket Required
13	Rapture
14	…And Justice For All
17	Brothers in Arms
19	Songs from the Big Chair
21	1984
23	Don't Be Cruel
24	Rhythm Nation 1814
25	Licensed to Ill
26	17
28	Hysteria
29	Like a Virgin
30	Metal Health
31	Synchronicity
32	Can't Slow Down
33	Thriller

DOWN

1	Escape
2	Invisible Touch
5	She's So Unusual
7	Eliminator
9	Kick
10	Slippery When Wet
11	Graceland
15	Hi Infidelity
16	An Innocent Man
18	So
20	4
22	Kick
27	Back in Black

GENERAL KNOWLEDGE 12

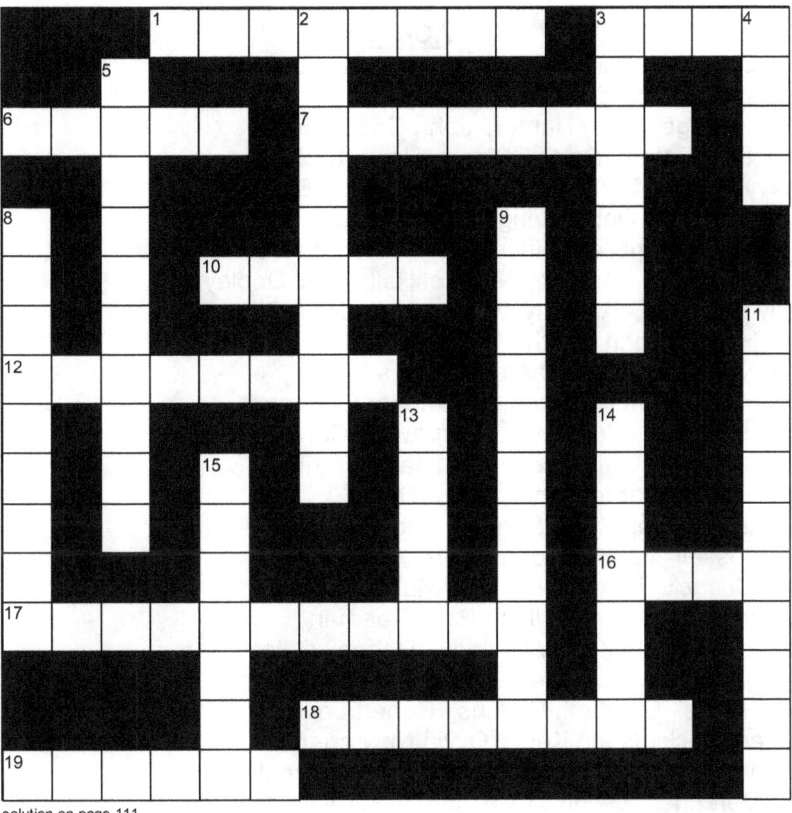

solution on page 111

ACROSS

1 1980 screwball comedy with Chevy Chase and Goldie Hawn, "Seems Like ___ _____"

3 Bully played by Thomas F. Wilson across three "Back to the Future" films

6 Kurt Russell's "Escape From New York" antihero, _____ Plissken

7 In "Smokey and the Bandit II," Bandit and Snowman are tasked with transporting "Charlotte" to Miami. What is Charlotte?

10 Band featured in 1980's concert film "Rockshow"

12 Stage name of Berry Gordy's son, who had a hit with "Somebody's Watching Me"

16 1981 film in which military cadets take over their school to save it from closing.

17 Introduced in 1981, Stouffer's frozen entrees that were low fat and lower calories

18 From "A Christmas Story," – *Be sure to drink your ________* "

19 Emilio Estevez's "Breakfast Club" character, the "jock"

DOWN

2 This band had another big hit with their 1987 cover of "Hazy Shade of Winter"

3 This band broke out with the release of their third album, 1986's "Slippery When Wet"

4 This company released the QuickSnap disposable camera in 1986

5 Denzel Washington's film debut, in which he meets his long lost father – played by George Segal

8 Ukrainian city; site of a major nuclear power plant disaster in 1986

9 Heavy metal band accused of putting subliminal messages in their songs

11 1980 sports comedy with Chevy Chase, Rodney Dangerfield, and Bill Murray

13 1986 revolution in this country led to the ousting of President Jean Claude Duvalier

14 1981 Jack Nicholson noir film remake, "The _____ Always Rings Twice"

15 Despite being a flop, this 1985 beverage actually ended up strengthening the market share of its brand

3 ACTORS IN A MOVIE 2

ACROSS

1 Kate Capshaw, Lea Thompson, Joaquin Phoenix
4 Madonna, Griffin Dunne, Haviland Morris
8 Nicolas Cage, Holly Hunter, John Goodman
9 Mark Linn-Baker, Peter O'Toole, Joseph Bologna
10 Chevy Chase, Beverly D'Angelo, Christie Brinkley
12 John Travolta, Debra Winger, Scott Glenn
15 Al Pacino, Michelle Pfeiffer, Mary Elizabeth Mastrantonio
16 Molly Ringwald, Anthony Michael Hall, Paul Dooley
17 Molly Ringwald, Anthony Michael Hall, Paul Gleason
19 Tom Hanks, John Candy, Daryl Hannah
21 Paul Newman, Jack Warden, James Mason
26 Tom Hanks, Shelley Long, Alexander Godunov
28 Molly Ringwald, Jon Cryer, Andrew McCarthy
29 Tim Robbins, Kevin Costner, Susan Sarandon
30 Tom Hanks, Carrie Fisher, Bruce Dern
31 Michael Keaton, Kim Basinger, Jack Nicholson
33 Kurt Russell, Jack Warden, Gerrit Graham
35 John Cusack, Ione Skye, John Mahoney
36 Harrison Ford, Karen Allen, Paul Freeman
38 Matthew Broderick, Ally Sheedy, Dabney Coleman
39 Jack Nicholson, Kathleen Turner, Anjelica Huston
40 Tom Hanks, Elizabeth Perkins, Robert Loggia
42 Michael Beck, Gene Kelly, Olivia Newton-John
43 Griffin Dunne, Rosanna Arquette, Linda Fiorentino
45 Tom Berenger, Glenn Close, Jeff Goldblum
46 Timothy Hutton, Donald Sutherland, Elizabeth McGovern
47 Andrew McCarthy, Jonathan Silverman, Catherine Mary Stewart
48 Corey Haim, Corey Feldman, Heather Graham

DOWN

1 Steve Guttenberg, Michael Winslow, Kim Cattrall
3 Matthew Broderick, Morgan Freeman, Denzel Washington
5 Christopher Guest, Michael McKean, Harry Shearer
6 Henry Fonda, Katherine Hepburn, Jane Fonda
7 Michael Keaton, Shelley Long, Henry Winkler
11 John Malkovich, Uma Thurman, Glenn Close
13 Kurt Russell, Goldie Hawn, Edward Herrmann
14 Lily Tomlin, Jane Fonda, Dolly Parton
18 Matthew Modine, R. Lee Ermey, Vincent D'Onofrio
19 Wil Wheaton, River Phoenix, Corey Feldman
20 Ethan Hawke, River Phoenix, Amanda Peterson
22 Gene Hackman, Dennis Hopper, Barbara Hershey
23 Emilio Estevez, Kiefer Sutherland, Lou Diamond Phillips
24 Goldie Hawn, Eileen Brennan, Armand Assante
25 Dan Aykroyd, John Belushi, Ray Charles
27 Kevin Bacon, Daniel Stern, Mickey Rourke
32 Michael Keaton, Teri Garr, Martin Mull
34 Bill Murray, Dan Aykroyd, Harold Ramis

36 Sylvester Stallone, Dolly Parton, Tim Thomerson
37 Chevy Chase, Dan Aykroyd, Bernie Mac
41 Harrison Ford, Kelly McGillis, Danny Glover
44 Robin Williams, Shelley Duvall, Ray Walston

solution on page 111

GENERAL KNOWLEDGE 13

solution on page 111

ACROSS

2 Michelle Pfeiffer lived on a diet of "Marlboros and tomato soup" while filming this 1983 crime movie.

7 The highest selling album of the 1980s, and it *isn't even close*.

10 Musician who won an Academy Award for "Arthur's Theme," Christopher _____

11 Irish artist, formerly of Clannad, who had major success with "Watermark"

12 According to Tommy Tutone, who would you reach by dialing 867-5309?

13 This 1983 film, set in a juvenile detention center, was the first film for Ally Sheedy, Clancy Brown, and Alan Ruck,

15 Name of the Jackson's 1984 concert tour

16 Laurence Fishburne's character on "Pee Wee's Playhouse," _______ Curtis

19 Kevin Costner's 1st film, "_____ Beach, USA"

20 Company that dominated the US home computer market in the 1980s with their VIC-20, 64, and 128 models

21 Type of candy bar used by Betelgeuse to lure a fly in "Beetlejuice"

DOWN

1 Nickname given to teen actors in the early 80s, the _____ Pack

3 English rock band that found success with the song "(I Just) Died in Your Arms"

4 Ten-week battle in 1982 between Argentina and the UK, the _________ War

5 Drew Barrymore's character in "E.T."

6 Wilhelm von Hornburg appeared in "Ghostbusters 2" as _____ the Carpathian

8 Launched in the US in 1980, this drink is packaged in a laminated foil vacuum pouch

9 Orson Welles' final performance was on this show, in an introduction to the 1985 episode entitled "The Dream Sequence Always Rings Twice"

14 Name of the haunted hotel in "The Shining"

17 In "Return of the Jedi," the shield generator for the second Death Star was located on the forest moon of _____.

18 After a five-year hiatus from releasing music, this singer/actress found success with a 1987 self-titled album and the single "I Found Someone"

HORROR MOVIES 2

solution on page 111

ACROSS

6 1984 film in which Contaminated Hazard Urban Disposal leads to Cannibalistic Humanoid Underground Dwellers

8 1982 John Carpenter remake of the 1951 classic that featured James Arness in the title role

9 1986 horror comedy in which Sonny Bono is turned into a pod by a powerful wizard

12 1984 Wes Craven-directed supernatural film that launched a major horror franchise

15 1988 remake of a 1958 Steve McQueen film

17 1987 John Carpenter film about an ancient cylinder found in a Los Angeles monastery

18 1983 adaptation of a Stephen King novel, starred Christopher Walken and Martin Sheen

20 1985 horror-comedy based on a short story by H. P. Lovecraft

21 1985 movie about little monsters, most notable for its poster showing one of them popping out of a toilet

DOWN

1 1988 John Carpenter film that tapped into his dissatisfaction with Ronald Reagan's economic policies and the commercialization of politics. Also, had a **bonkers** fight scene.

2 1984 Stephen King adaptation featuring "He Who Walks Behind the Rows"

3 1986 film about a teen haunted by the ghost of his rock hero. Cameos by Gene Simmons and Ozzy Osbourne

4 Third film in George Romero's "Dead" series

5 1982 remake of a 1942 film, starring Nastassja Kinski and Malcolm McDowell

7 This 1989 adaptation of a Stephen King novel opines "sometimes, dead is better."

10 1988 film about the lone survivor of a mass suicide, haunted by the ghost of its leader

11 1981 slasher with Linda Blair about a night of fraternity hazing that goes awry

13 1983 summer camp slasher film that is notorious for its twist ending

14 1986 Irish horror film, based on a Clive Barker story, about a pagan deity monster

18 1982 cult classic about a guy who carries his telepathic conjoined twin around New York City in a wicker basket.

19 Absolute classic 1986 sequel to a 1979 film about a xenomorph infestation on a distant planet. Admittedly, this one's way more action than horror but it still counts

GRAMMY AWARDS

<u>ACROSS</u>

3 He won 1982's Best Country Vocal (male) for "Always on My Mind"

4 He won 1988's Album of the Year for "Faith"

8 Danny Elfman won 1989's Best Instrumental Composition for the theme from this movie

9 Supergroup that recorded 1985's Song of the Year "We Are the World"

11 1983s Album of the Year, which featured the song in 19-across

12 The Highwaymen, a country supergroup, won Best Country Song for this 1985 song (which inspired their name)

13 This release by John Lennon and Yoko Ono won Best Album of 1981

15 Bette Midler won record and Song of the Year in 1989 for a song from this movie.

16 Olivia Newton-John won the Video of the Year award in 1983 for this video

18 1981's Record and Song of the Year went to her song "Bette Davis Eyes"

19 1983's Record of the Year went to Michael Jackson for this song

21 Winner of 1985's Album of the Year for his third solo album, "No Jacket Required"

22 1981's Grammy or Best Country Vocal (female) went to this singer of "9 to 5"

26 With Lionel Richie, credited songwriter for 8-across

28 Jan Hammer won 1985's Best Instrumental Composition for this theme

29 This artist won 1988's Song, Record, and Pop Performance of the Year for "Don't Worry, Be Happy"

32 In 1983, this Canadian country-pop singer won her fourth Grammy Award for "A Little Good News"

35 This Australian band won 1982's Best New Artist

36 At the end of the day, this show won 1987's Best Musical Cast Show Album

37 He won the Best Comedy award two years in a row for "Rev. Du Rite" and "Live on the Sunset Strip"

38 In 1985, this "Girl's Just Want to Have Fun" singer won Best New Artist

39 1984's Record and Song of the Year went to her for "What's Love Got to Do With It?"

40 This mother-daughter duo won Best Group Country Performance in 1985, 1986, 1987, and 1989

<u>DOWN</u>

1 The Oak Ridge Boys won Best Group Country Performance for their version of this 1966 Dallas Frazier song

2 Paul Simon won 1987's Album of the Year and 1988's Record of the Year for this title. Sounds weird, doesn't it?

5 Steve Winwood won 1986's Record of the Year for this song

6 This artist won 1980's Record of the Year, Album of the Year, Song of the Year, *and* Best New Artist. He was the first artist to win all four of the "main" awards.

7 She won Best Gospel Performance (female) in 1983, 1984, and 1985

10 The Police won 1983's Best Group Rock Performance for this song (from the album of the same name)

14 She won 1988's Best Female Pop Performance for "Fast Car"

17 He won 1984's Album of the Year for "Can't Slow Down" (which featured Song of the Year nominee "Hello")

20 U2 won 1987's Album of the Year for this release, which featured "I Still Haven't Found What I'm Looking For"

23 This composer won three Grammy Awards for his work on "E.T. the Extra-Terrestrial"

24 This duet from "An American Tail" won 1987's Song of the Year

25 This soundtrack won "Best Comedy Album" of 1988, despite containing only six minutes of comedy material.

27 Merle Haggard won Best Male Country Vocal for his 1984 remake of "That's the Way _____ Goes"

30 Toto won 1982's Record of the Year for this song (and no, it's NOT "Africa")

31 Weird Al Yankovic won his first Grammy award for this 1984 song

33 He won Best Country Vocal (male) two years in a row with "Always and Forever" and "Old 8x10"

34 She won 1989's Album of the Year for "Nick of Time"

GRAMMY AWARDS

Use the clues on the previous page!

solution on page 112

HIP-HOP

solution on page 111

ACROSS

1 This group toured with Madonna to promote their album "Licensed to Ill"

6 Their debut album "3 Feet and Rising" featured the #1 R&B hit "Me Myself and I"

8 "The Breaks" from his 1980 debut album, is the first rap song to be certified a gold record.

11 Their album "Criminal Minded" is considered one of the earliest examples of gangsta rap

12 Their breakthrough album "Crushin'" featured a cover of "Wipe Out" featuring the Beach Boys

14 His 1985 song "P.S.K. What Does It Mean" is considered the first gangsta rap song

15 Funk-fueled sample-heavy group with popular tracks "You Gots to Chill" and "Strictly Business"

16 His 1987 debut album, "Rhyme Pays," featured the single "6 in the Mornin'"

20 With the Get Fresh Crew, this "human beat box" had success with track "The Show"

21 Though the song came out in 1979, the Sugarhill Gang were sure to put this hit on their 1980 debut

23 The "clown prince of Hip Hop," he had a breakthrough hit with 1989's "Just a Friend"

DOWN

2 A founding member of N.W.A., this west coast rapper had solo success with "Eazy-Duz-It"

3 Pioneers in sampling, their debut "Critical Beatdown," featured songs "Ego Trippin'" and "Traveling at the Speed of Thought"

4 "Straight Outta Compton" band that featured Ice Cube, Dr, Dre, and others

5 This member of the Juice Crew had success with "Ain't No Half-Steppin'"

7 Def Jam's first full-length album release was his debut, featuring "Rock the Bells"

9 Band whose cover of "Walk This Way" charted higher than the original version

10 Their song "Magic's Wand" was the first rap song accompanied by a music video.

13 The _______ War was a mid-80s rivalry, started by a 14-year-old girl's diss track

17 1980 release by the Treacherous Three; one of the first to mix hip-hop and rock and roll.

18 Rivalry during the mid-to-late 1980s about the birthplace of hip hop, the _______ Wars

19 Her 1988 album "Lyte as a Rock" was the first full album released by a female rapper.

22 New York group started by Chuck D and Flavor Flav in 1985

GENERAL KNOWLEDGE 14

solution on page 112

ACROSS

1 1987 Best Picture winner, "The Last ______"

5 1980 Woody Allen film that parodies Fellini's "8½," "________ Memories"

10 Known for Bud Light commercials, Spuds Mackenzie was this breed of dog

11 Furry inhabitants of the forest moon of Endor who are never named in "Return of the Jedi"

13 Annie ______, played Janine the receptionist in "Ghostbusters"

16 This type of Ray Ban sunglasses became very popular after the release of "Top Gun"

17 John Lennon and Yoko One's 1980 album, "Double ________"

18 Name of the girl created by "little maniacs" Gary and Wyatt in "Weird Science"

19 William Conrad crime show, in which he played a D.A. , "___ and the Fatman"

20 The climax of "Do the Right Thing" includes the destruction of _____ Pizzeria

DOWN

2 Aired in 1983, the series finale of this show remains the most watched scripted television show of all time

3 1981 film with Sylvester Stallone and Michael Caine, in which Allied POWs play a football match against a German team.

4 Surname of actor who played Cash in "Tango and Cash"

6 1982 hit song by Toto, famously covered (*but not improved**) by Weezer in 2018

7 In 1980, The World Health Assembly declared this disease eradicated.

8 1981 fantasy adventure with Sean Connery appearing as King Agamemnon

9 David Lee Roth's 1985 song, "Just a ______"

12 Texas child who fell in a well, Baby ______

13 Robin Williams landed his first leading role in this 1980 comic adaptation

14 This 1980 horror film reunited Jamie Lee Curtis with "Halloween" director John Carpenter

15 This country adopted its own constitution and became independent of the UK in 1982

** yeah, I said it.*

ACTION MOVIES 2

solution on page 112

ACROSS

5 Kurt Russell is an ex-soldier and federal prisoner who has to rescue the President

10 Steven Seagal's first film; he plays a Chicago cop embroiled in CIA shenanigans

13 Michael Pare is a mercenary hired to rescue his ex-girlfriend from a motorcycle gang led by Willem Dafoe in this "Rock & Roll Fable"

15 Post-apocalyptic Jean-Claude van Damme flick, infamously thrown together by its producers when He Man 2 fell apart

16 Teenage guerillas fight in Soviet occupied Colorado in this 1984 World War 3 film

18 A group of elite soldiers are picked off one-by-one by an alien hunter in the jungle.

19 An imprisoned Vietnam vet is offered his freedom if he returns to Vietnam to search for POWs. He isn't supposed to engage the enemy. Yeah, right.

20 Roy Scheider is a pilot fighting a conspiracy involving a prototype helicopter

21 A robot from the future is sent back in time to kill the mother of the leader of the resistance.

DOWN

1 1982 film that spawned a franchise which includes the film in 19-across

2 Eric Roberts and James Earl Jones star in this 1989 marital arts film

3 Louis Gossett Jr. helps a young pilot on a rescue mission to save his father.

4 1983 epic fantasy film starring Arnold Schwarzenegger and James Earl Jones

6 A romance novelist travels to Colombia in an attempt to save her kidnapped sister

7 Michael Douglas and Andy Garcia are NYC cops who must escort a member of the Yakuza to Japan.

8 Clint Eastwood plays an aging Marine who must lead a platoon into Grenada

9 Two LA cops are framed for murder by crime lord Jack Palance

11 1989 John Woo film about an assassin trying to earn money to help an innocent victim

12 1987 buddy cop film with Danny Glover and Mel Gibson

14 1986 film featuring the climax of an ancient war between immortal sword fighting warriors

COMEDY MOVIES 2

solution on page 112

ACROSS

1 1983 classic based on stories in two books by humorist Jean Shephard

5 1984 black comedy starring Nick Nolte about the goings-on at a Columbus high school

7 1982 musical in which Julie Andrews dresses as a man so she can pretend to be a man who's impersonating a woman. Wait, what?

10 A bounty hunter pursues a Mafia accountant while being chased by the F.B.I., the mob, and another bounty hunter.

11 A prudish couple rob and kill wealthy swingers to help fund their dream restaurant

13 A popular high school student totally didn't pass out last night at 31 Flavors so no, Simone *I don't think it's that serious*.

15 Rodney Dangerfield must lose weight and give up drugs and gambling if he wants to receive a $10 million inheritance.

18 The new owner of the Cleveland Indians loads the team with losers in an attempt to relocate to Miami.

20 A cocktail waitress prevents an assassination and accidentally becomes a national heroine

21 Goldie Hawn plays a spoiled young woman who is duped into joining the Army.

DOWN

2 1984 mockumentary following one of England's loudest bands.

3 A Detroit police officer travels to Los Angeles to solve a friend's murder

4 Due to a police shortage, a city changes its policy to accept all recruit applications. Does the motley crew have what it takes?

6 Mel Brooks' 1987 parody of all things space related (but mostly Star Wars)

8 This 1988 comedy is based on the short-lived television series "Police Squad!"

9 Mel Brooks and Anne Bancroft star in this remake of a 1942 WW2-set film.

12 This pirate film, the final film of both Marty Feldman and Spike Mulligan, also featured several Monty Python members and Cheech and Chong

14 Chevy Chase plays a journalist with a habit of wearing disguises

18 Steve Martin stars in a modern interpretation of "Cyrano de Bergerac"

17 A dying millionaire's soul is accidentally transferred into her lawyer, Steve Martin

19 Richard Pryor plays a man who has to relocate his family for work. Hijinks ensue.

GENERAL KNOWLEDGE 15

solution on page 112

ACROSS

1 Michael J. Fox's first film appearance was in this 1980 comedy about a college competitive game, "Midnight _______"

5 Steve Martin plays Dr. Michael Hfuhruhurr in "The Man with Two ______"

6 Michael _______, billed as The Man of 10,000 Sound Effects, appeared in "Spaceballs" and "Police Academy"

8 This supertanker hit an Alaskan reef in 1989, causing a massive oil spill

11 Sam J. Jones beat out Kurt Russell and Arnold Schwarzenegger for the lead role in this 1980 space opera

15 "I am serious, and don't call me _______"

16 1980 Siouxsie and the Banshees song about a woman with Multiple Personality Disorder

17 Canadian sketch comedy show, hosted by John Byner, that was aired in the US on the Showtime network

18 Rolling Stones bassist who married his girlfriend *of six years* when she turned 19. I'm sorry, what?

DOWN

2 1982 comedy-drama following a close-knit group of friends in 1959 Baltimore

3 Leader of a group of ~~petty~~ exceptional thieves in "Die Hard," Hans _____

4 Forest Whitaker stars in this 1988 biopic of jazz musician Charlie Parker

6 Pop duo consisting of George Michael and Andrew Ridgeley

7 Edie Brickell and the New Bohemians had a 1988 hit with this anti-philosophical song

9 Terry Kiser spends the majority of a 1989 film playing this titular dead guy.

10 This pioneer of reggae passed away in 1980 after a long fight with skin cancer

12 This actor lampooned his 1979 appearance in "Alien" by falling victim to yet another chestburster in "Spaceballs"

13 Played by Carrie Henn, this young girl was the only survivor of the Hadley's Hope settlement in "Aliens"

14 This handheld gaming system debuted in 1989 to massive sales thanks in part to being packaged with "Tetris"

ROMANCE MOVIES

solution on page 113

ACROSS

2 A low-level secretary pretends to be her boss; does a better job and *steals her boyfriend*

6 Robert Downey, Jr. plays a man who is killed in a car accident, then comes back and dates his own daughter. Yeah, it's complicated.

8 John Cusack and Daphne Zuniga fall for each other on the road trip from hell

9 When he's not throwing booze bottles around like a damned maniac, bartender Tom Cruise tries to woo Elisabeth Shue.

11 Holly Hunter Is an intense news producer who is attracted to William Hurt, much to the chagrin of reporter Albert Brooks

12 John Cusack and a boombox. If you don't already know this, you're in the wrong book.

13 Molly Ringwald is torn between a preppy boy and her social outcast best friend,

14 An actor falls in love with his costar, but she thinks he's a woman. It happens.

16 A young woman in the Catskills falls in love with her dance instructor,

17 Rob Lowe and Demi Moore star in this 1986 film based on David Mamet's play "Sexual Perversity in Chicago"

18 Richard Dreyfus plays a dead man who helps a living guy hook up with his girlfriend.

19 Brooke Shields and Christopher Atkins play two shipwrecked teenagers who fall in love

20 A playwright goes back in time via self-hypnosis to woo an actress in 1912

DOWN

1 Robert Downey, Jr. plays a womanizer who meets his match in Molly Ringwald

2 Billy Crystal and Meg Ryan are two acquaintances who come in and out of each other's lives over twelve years

3 An Egyptian princess from 2514 BC comes to life as a 1987 window display

4 Brooks Shields has to break up with her boyfriend, who then burns down her house. *And there's still like an hour to go!*

5 A farmhand must rescue his true love from a dastardly prince.

7 Tom Hanks falls in love with a mysterious woman who is an excellent swimmer

10 Patrick Dempsey plays a nerd who pays a cheerleader $1,000 to pose as his girlfriend and I guarantee you that this is NOT what the Beatles were singing about.

15 Steve Martin is a fire chief who tries to help a coworker woo Daryl Hannah, only to fall in love with her himself

THE FIRE

In 1989, Billy Joel released the song "We Didn't Start the Fire." Now you get to relive the fun that was the homework where you had to explain all the references contained in the song.

<u>ACROSS</u>

1 Automaker that merged with Packard in 1954; ceased production ten years later

8 Spanish-American philosopher; died 1952

10 Amusement Park that opened in 1955

14 Hollywood bombshell who appeared in "Gentlemen Prefer Blondes"

16 Premier of the Soviet Union 1958 - 1964

18 Singer who dominated the charts in the late 50s with songs like "Love Me Tender"

24 1958 car released by Ford which flopped

28 Term for the intense fandom surrounding the lads from Liverpool

29 Boxer who defeated Jake LaMotta in 1951

32 Site where the Korean Armistice Agreement was signed in 1953

33 Roy __________, one of major league baseball's first black athletes

34 Leader of Soviet Union in-between 15-down and 16-across

35 Political scandal involving 50-across

37 Scandal in which radio DJs took bribes to promote certain songs

41 Rocky _________, world heavyweight boxing champ from 1952 – 1956

42 Developer of the theory of relativity, this German-born physicist died in 1955

45 Morning sickness drug pulled from market because it caused fetal deformities

46 Nazi official who was executed in 1962 for his extensive role in the Holocaust

47 Couple who was the first American citizens executed for espionage

48 1951 Rodgers and Hammerstein musical about a teacher and the King of Siam

49 In 1983, she became the first US woman to fly in space

50 Disgraced US president, 1969 – 1974

52 Political leader of Cuba from 1959 – 2008

53 Beat Generation author, released "On the Road" in 1957

54 Leader of South Korea, forced to resign in 1960

55 Flamboyant pianist, had a television variety program from 1952 – 1969

<u>DOWN</u>

1 Egypt took control of this artificial waterway in 1956, sparking a crisis.

2 Singer who released hits "Peggy Sue" and "That'll Be the Day," died in 1959

3 Rock and Roll star in the early 50s, considered "Elvis before Elvis"

4 1960 classic Hitchcock film about a boy and his mother

5 Actress deemed the "French Sex Kitten"

6 High strength texture fiber used in medical procedures, debuted in 1951

7 1956 novel by Grace Metalious

9 England's new queen, circa 1953

11 Country that invaded South Korea in 1950

12 Hollywood star who left her career in 1956 to marry the Prince of Monaco

13 Arkansas governor involved in messy, overpublicized divorce in 1954

15 Leader of the Soviet Union from 1924 until 1953

17 His "The Twist" was a hit and dance sensation in 1960

19 Italian conductor who died in 1957

20 "Peter and the Wolf" composer; died 1953

21 Heartthrob actor, star of "Rebel Without a Cause," died in a car crash at 24

22 State in which Rosa Parks refused to give up her bus seat

23 1957 war film about men imprisoned in a Japanese POW camp

25 Chief counsel for 31-down

26 This acclaimed author of "A Farewell to Arms" committed suicide in 1961

27 Hollywood star from "A Streetcar Named Desire" and others, Marlon _______

30 1954 hit by Bill Haley and the Comets

31 Wisconsin senator who led the 1950s communist witch hunt

36 Beloved actress who appeared in "Pillow Talk," "The Man Who Knew Too Much"

38 Brooklyn's winning team

39 1959 biblical epic with Charlton Heston

40 TV series with Fess Parker

43 US president, 1953 - 1961

44 Failed 1961 invasion of Cuba landed at this location on the south-central coast

51 He led Egypt's revolution in 1952; would become prime minister and president

THE FIRE

Use the clues over on page 66

solution on page 113

By the way, this was all much harder back in the day when we had to use encyclopedias!

GENERAL KNOWLEDGE 16

solution on page 113

ACROSS

5 In his 1986-87 season, this member of the Chicago Bulls scored over 3,000 points

6 ABC drama about wealthy Colorado families, a direct competitor to CBS' "Dallas"

8 1981 sports drama, "__________ of Fire"

10 1985 sci-fi film with Dennis Quaid and Louis Gossett, Jr., "Enemy ____"

13 1985 Phil Collins album, "No ____ Required"

14 This Andrew Lloyd-Webber musical made its Broadway debut in 1982 at the Winter Garden Theatre

15 This movie chronicles two offspring of a secret 1953 genetics test combining the DNA of six fathers to produce a child.

16 In "Ferris Bueller's Day Off," Cameron is entranced by a painting by this French artist

17 Microsoft operating system launched in 1985

19 This singer had 99 problems and they were all luftballoons

20 Meryl Streep stars in this 1983 drama about a nuclear whistleblower

21 This member of the Four Tops voiced Audrey II in "Little Shop of Horrors"

22 Name of Pee-Wee's dog in "Pee-Wee's Big Adventure"

DOWN

1 1986 public fundraising event, "_____ Across America"

2 The CDC recognized this as a new disease on September 24, 1982

3 1987 Bruce Willis album, "The Return of ______"

4 California resort city in which Sonny Bono was mayor from 1988 to 1992

7 1984 Richard Gere crime drama centering on a Harlem jazz club in the 1930s

9 Stephen Sondheim musical that opened in 1987 with Bernadette Peters as a witch

11 Orson Welles narrated "The Man Who Saw Tomorrow," a documentary about this astrologer and reputed seer

12 English rock band that relaunched itself to great success in 1987 with hits like "Here I Go Again" and "Is This Love"

18 The second-highest grossing album of the 80s (and of all time), AC/DC's "Back in ____"

POP MUSIC

solution on page 114

ACROSS

1 Billy Jean
2 Don't Talk to Strangers
3 We Don't Need Another Hero
6 Flashdance (What a Feeling)
8 Wrapped Around Your Finger
10 Wake Me Up Before You Go-Go
11 Do You Really Want to Hurt Me?
13 Don't You (Forget About Me)
15 Jump
18 Every Rose Has Its Thorn
19 Saving All My Love for You
22 Girls Just Wanna Have Fun
23 Dancing in the Dark
24 Father Figure
25 Little Red Corvette
26 I Love Rock & Roll
28 Material Girl
29 True
30 Shout
31 The Search is Over

DOWN

1 Who Can It Be Now?
2 Never Gonna Give You Up
3 Sweet Dreams (Are Made of This)
4 Fast Car
5 You Shook Me All Night Long
7 Don't Stop Believin'
9 Hello
12 In the Air Tonight
14 Hungry Like the Wolf
16 Another One Bites the Dust
17 Funkytown
19 Here I Go Again
20 Walk Like an Egyptian
21 We Got the Beat
27 Africa

MTV

solution on page 113

ACROSS

2 This British comedy starring Rik Mayall was the first non-music related program MTV aired

5 Premiered in 1987; videos from heavy metal bands were played on "_____________Ball"

6 1970s British sketch troupe whose show often aired in blocks with 2-across

9 Premiered in 1986; videos from alternative music bands were shown on "120 ________"

13 "Just Say Julie" was a late-night show starring comedienne Julie _____, not to be confused with the one from Downtown

14 Easy one – the first video on MTV was "Video Killed the Radio Star" by this band

16 Original Veejay, J.J. ________

17 Original Veejay, _____ Blackwood

18 Original Veejay, _____ Hunter

20 Hosted by Ken Ober, this was MTV's first foray into game shows

21 The show "15 Minutes" featured this pop artist interviewing other celebrities. Also, the show ran 30 minutes, so…false advertising, right?

22 MTV ran 16 hours of this 1985 benefit concert (with limited commercial interruptions, of course)

DOWN

1 Only viewers in this state saw the network when it started broadcasting

2 Winners of MTV's first Best Video Award for 1984's "You Might Think"

3 Christopher Connelly hosted this weekly show previewing upcoming movies

4 The 1989 first episode of this show featured Squeeze, Syd Straw, and Elliot Easton

7 Okay, so you knew 14-across. What singer had the *second* video on MTV?

8 This artist's career blew up after her performance in wedding attire at the first VMA

9 Original Veejay, _____ Goodman

10 This pop band had a massive resurgence in 1986 when MTV aired a marathon of their 1966-1968 television show

11 Premiered in 1988, videos from hip hop artists were shown on "Yo! MTV _____"

12 Original Veejay, Martha ______

15 This band may have inspired 4-down when they performed an acoustic version of their song "Wanted Dead or Alive" at the 1989 VMA show.

19 Occasional comedy show in which "Weird Al" Yankovic commandeers the network

GENERAL KNOWLEDGE 17

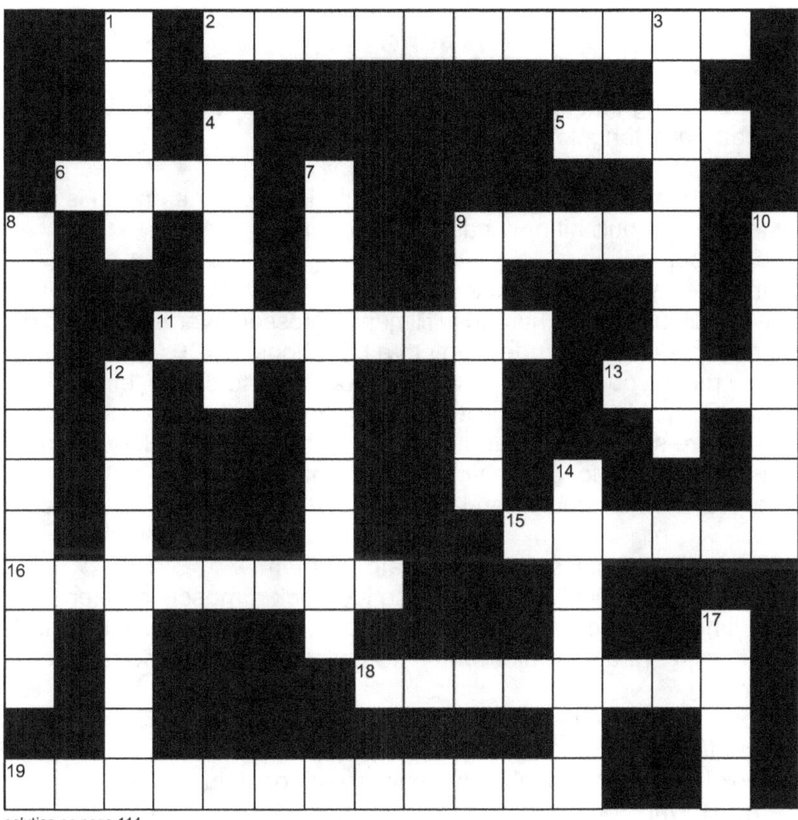

solution on page 114

ACROSS

2 Sam Raimi's 1981 iconic horror film, based on his short "Within the Woods"

5 Launched in 1989, this reality show followed police officers at work

6 1981 prehistoric fantasy film starring Rae Dawn Chong, "Quest for _____"

9 This 1982 musical adaptation featured Albert Finney and Carol Burnett

11 Fictional club located on Pico Boulevard in Los Angeles where Reese first saves Sarah Connor from the terminator

13 Dickless EPA official who screws up everything at Ghostbusters HQ, Walter _____

15 1985 Timothy Hutton / Sean Penn spy drama, "The _____ & the Snowman"

16 1984 game for the Nintendo Entertainment System that used the NES Zapper

18 This woman closes out the list in The Nails' song "88 Lines About 44 Women"

19 He won the NHL MVP award every year from 1979 through 1987. Then he came back and got it again for the 1988/89 season

DOWN

1 "The _____ and Max Devlin" was considered controversial in 1981 because Bill Cosby played a villain. *Yeah, y'all can go ahead and make your own joke here.*

3 This chain restaurant opened its first location in Atlanta, Georgia in 1980.

4 Judd Nelson's "Breakfast Club" character, John _____ ("the criminal")

7 This English actor earned the adoration of a generation when he played P. I. Eddie Valiant in "Who Framed Roger Rabbit"

8 This Central American country was involved in a Civil War throughout the 1980s

9 Lance Henriksen plays an android – sorry, *synthetic person*, in this 1986 classic

10 Woodbridge Township, New Jersey made headlines in 1982 when it banned public usage of this Sony product

12 Gene Wilder and Richard Pryor are mistaken for bank robbers in this film

14 Host city of the 1988 Winter Olympics

17 This Indonesian-Dutch singer had a hit in 1982 with a cover of "Puttin' on the Ritz"

MOVIE QUOTES 2

ACROSS

3 He's a real gentleman! I bet he takes the dishes out of the sink before he pees in it.
5 Do you ever get the feeling that there's something going on that we don't know about?
7 I can hold my breath for a long, long time!
8 Oh, no tears, please. It's a waste of good suffering.
13 I'm an insect who dreamt he was a man and loved it. But now the dream is over
15 Dear diary, my teen angst bullshit now has a body count.
18 If you build it, he will come.
22 I think now, looking back, we did not fight the enemy; we fought ourselves. And the enemy was in us.
25 My name is Joel Goodsen. I deal in human fulfillment. I grossed over 8 thousand dollars in one night.
31 My minimum price for taking a stranded lady to a telephone is 400 dollars.
33 God wouldn't have given you maracas if he didn't want you to shake 'em.
35 You're a funny guy Sully, I like you. That's why I'm going to kill you last.
36 What did one shepherd say to the other shepherd? Let's get the flock out of here!
37 Why don't we just...Wait here for a little while? See what happens.
38 You said you wanted to be around when I made a mistake, well, this could be it, sweetheart.

DOWN

1 I am not a destroyer of companies. I am a liberator of them!
2 Her monthly bill came early. Well, she's fine, she just took a muscle relaxer.
4 You wanna waste time with a fictional character? I mean, you're a sweet girl. You deserve a human.
6 Why, my Uncle Thumper had a problem with HIS probate, and he had to take these big pills, and drink lots of water
9 In this country, you gotta make the money first. Then when you get the money, you get the power. Then when you get the power, then you get the women.
10 You know, you look like your head fell in the cheese dip back in 1957
11 I can't put my arms down!
12 I have foresworn myself. I have broken every law I have sworn to uphold, I have become what I beheld and I am content that I have done right!
14 Ok, I'll meet you at the place near the thing where we went that time.
16 You can't write comedy in California! It's not depressing enough
17 Excuse me. I have to go. Somewhere there is a crime happening.
19 Why are things so heavy in the future? Is there a problem with the Earth's gravitational pull?
20 Now they will know why they are afraid of the dark. Now they will learn why they fear the night.
21 Welcome to the Statue of Liberty. The Statue is a gift from French citizens and has come to symbolize hope for naked women everywhere.
23 We didn't start this, we didn't mean it to happen, but we're not givin' up til you pay. FAIR IS FAIR!
24 I could be the walrus. I'd still have to bum rides off people.
26 You know, this is the cleanest and nicest police car I've ever been in in my life. This thing's nicer than my apartment.
27 I can say 'hello' in a lot of different languages. Not yours, but a lot of them.
28 Hey, lady! It's against the rules to throw other peoples' heads!
29 I apologize for calling your wife a bloated warthog, and I bid you good day.
30 We need a live rooster to take the curse off Jose's glove and nobody seems to know what to get Millie or Jimmy for their wedding present.
32 Boys, you must strive to find your own voice. Because the longer you wait to begin, the less likely you are to find it at all.
34 Just a reminder, fans, comin' up is our "Die-hard Night" here at the stadium. Free admission to anyone who was actually alive the last time the Indians won a pennant.

MOVIE QUOTES 2

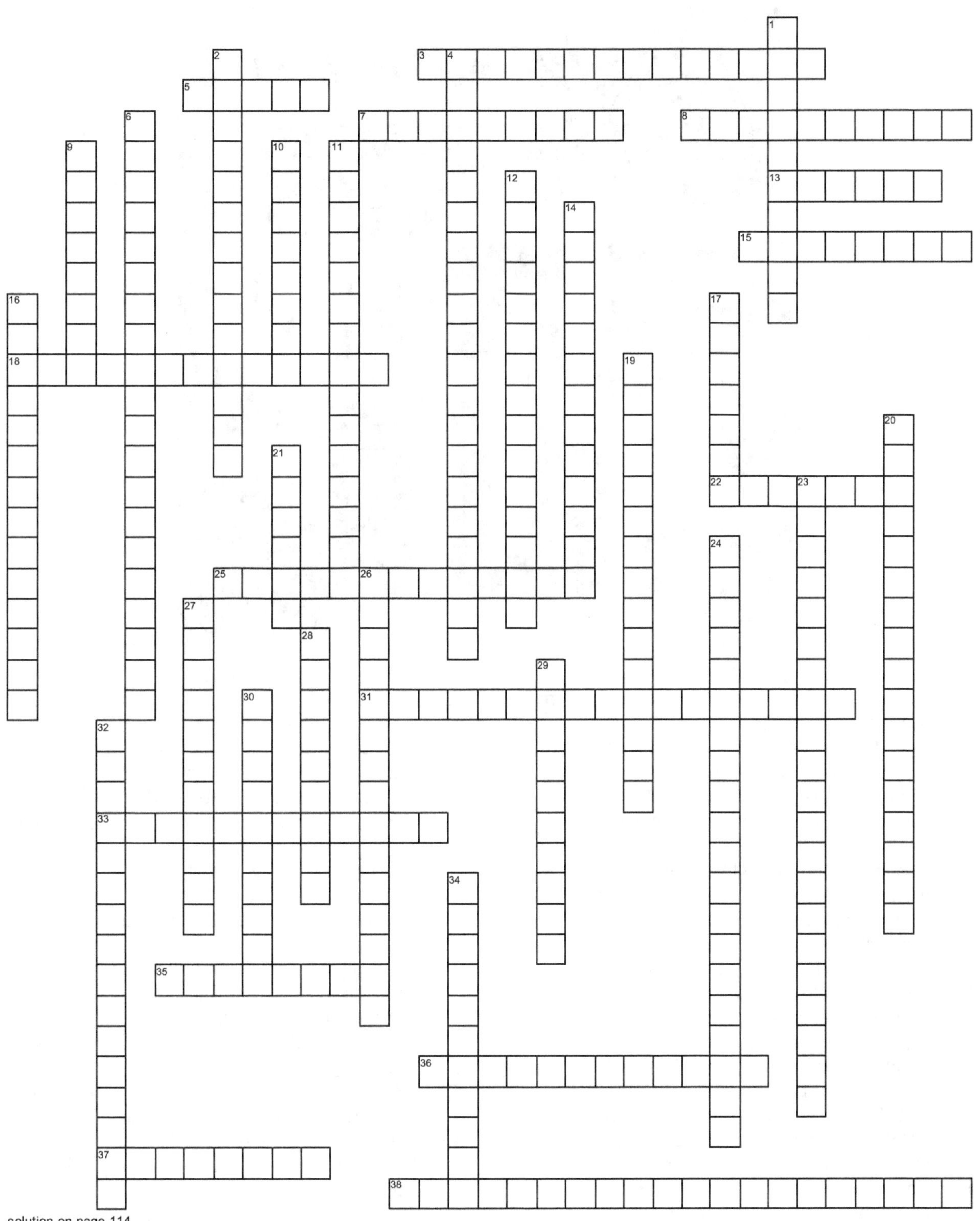

solution on page 114

GENERAL KNOWLEDGE 18

solution on page 114

ACROSS

1 Charity supergroup that recorded "We Are the World" in 1985

5 With 1982's "Valley Girl" this artist scored his first (and only) top-40 hit

8 1982 supernatural film in which Barbara Hershey is tormented by an invisible assailant

10 Ray Walston played this teacher (who thinks everyone is on dope) in "Fast Times and Ridgemont High"

14 Type of flower given to E.T. by Elliot's sister in "E.T. the Extra-Terrestrial"

15 Fashion trend invented when two men dyed fishermen's PVC footwear vivid colors, _____shoes

17 John Candy's Chewbacca-inspired character in "Spaceballs"

18 In 1985, an electrical engineer jammed this network's satellite signal in protest of them charging for their programming

19 This 1981 Thomas Harris novel marked the first appearance of Hannibal Lecter

DOWN

2 The Beastmaster's constant companions, Kodo and Podo, were this type of animal

3 Francis Ford Coppola directed this Michael Jackson 3D film, a 17-minute-long theme park attraction for Disney Parks

4 John Lennon was shot outside this famous New York apartment building, where he lived with Yoko Ono and his son Sean

6 Popular 1980's t-shirt "Frankie Say _____"

7 This musician played Baron Charles Frankenstein in 1986's "The Bride"

9 Tom Hanks and his buddies become convinced their new neighbors are part of a murderous cult in this film

11 This Robert Guillaume sitcom was a spin-off of the show "Soap"

12 Sold by Worlds of Wonder, this game used infrared guns and wearable targets

13 After winning his second Tour de France, he was the first cyclist to appear on the cover of Sports Illustrated

16 A glass pyramid structure designed by I.M. Pei opened at this museum in 1988.

MORE SONGS FROM THE ORIGINAL SOUNDTRACK

Once again, identify the movies in which these songs were prominently featured.

solution on page 115

ACROSS

2 Into the Groove
10 Scandalous
11 When Doves Cry
14 Who Wants to Live Forever?
16 It's in the Way That You Use It
19 Power of Love
20 (Don't You) Forget About Me
21 When the Going Gets Tough, the Tough Get Going
22 Sweet Freedom
23 After All
24 Hazy Shade of Winter

DOWN

1 Kokomo
3 Put a Little Love in Your Heart
4 Take My Breath Away
5 Maniac
6 Papa Can You Hear Me
7 Man in Motion
8 Rhythm of the Night
9 'Cause I'm a Blonde
10 Wind Beneath My Wings
12 The Heat is On
13 Old Time Rock and Roll
15 Live to Tell
17 Living in America
18 Nothing's Gonna Stop Us Now

GENERAL KNOWLEDGE 19

solution on page 115

ACROSS

2 1984 comedy superhero splatter film in which a tutu-wearing weakling becomes a deformed hero, "The _____ Avenger"

4 1988 stinker that somehow tried to pair "E.T." with a trip to McDonalds.

7 1981 Peter Falk film about a female wrestling tag team, "…All the ______"

10 "American ________," a 1989 competitive TV program pitting contestants against athletes with names like "Nitro" and "Zap"

11 This TV lawyer was known for his thriftiness and his love of hot dogs

13 This toy company launched its Micro Machines brand in 1986 to much success

18 This automobile executive's autobiography was the bestselling non-fiction hardback book of 1984 and 1985

19 In 1983, the United States embassy in this country was attacked by a suicide car bombing.

20 This former Disney animator opened his own studio, producing films like "The Secret of NIMH" and "An American Tail"

DOWN

1 1987 Eric Bogosian play about a shock jock on the brink of national syndication

3 This membership-only chain opened its first warehouse in 1983

5 1981's "The Great Muppet _____"

6 In 1988, this member of Creedence Clearwater Revival won a plagiarism lawsuit…against himself.

8 This 1989 film was based on the book that the play that "Dangerous Liaisons" was based on was based on. No, really.

9 Toni Basil's 1981 hit

12 Critically acclaimed 1988 French adventure film starring Bart and Youk.

14 Hockey team which, bolstered by Wayne Gretzky, won four Stanley Cups in the 80s

15 Cheese dip-loving Comic parody of Conan the Barbarian, "___ the Wanderer"

16 1986 David Lynch film prominently featuring a severed ear, "Blue ______"

17 Launched in 1983, this timepiece company intended their products to be casual and disposable accessories

SCI-FI MOVIES 2

Solution on Page 115

ACROSS

1 Tom Cruise must stop Tim Curry's Lord of Darkness from destroying daylight

3 Timothy Dalton and Brian Blessed costar in this 1980 adaptation of the King Features comic strip

7 A man who can enter people's dreams is recruited to help cure the President of his recurring apocalyptic nightmares.

8 1985 Terry Gilliam film about a bureaucratic nightmare future

10 A human soldier and an alien soldier must work together to survive after both crash on an inhospitable planet.

15 1981 Cronenberg film about a secret war between two groups of powerful psychics

16 Low budget 1980 film with Richard Thomas and John Saxon; "Seven Samurai" as a space opera

19 The idea for this movie came about when someone joked that Rocky had run out of human opponents, so he'd have to fight an alien next. Only difference is they got Arnold Schwarzenegger instead.

20 A programmer gets digitized and sucked into a computer mainframe

DOWN

2 An ex-solider must infiltrate the most dangerous city in the US to rescue the President from a terrorist group

4 Peter MacNicol is a young wizard's apprentice who is sent to fight a dragon.

5 A young man goes back in time and has to fight off his mother's advances (among other problems)

6 A drifter roams the post-apocalyptic wasteland in this 1981 Mad Max sequel

8 This loose adaptation of Greek mythology featured the final work of stop-motion legend Ray Harryhausen.

11 An anthropomorphic mallard is transported to Earth; hijinks ensue

13 Three boys build a dream-inspired space craft and go out in search of alien life.

14 A dead couple fight to protect their house from obnoxious city-folk.

17 There's a new sheriff in town. Oh, but the town is actually Jupiter's moon Io, and the sheriff is Sean Connery

18 A robot boy is adopted by a South Carolina family but hunted by the government agency that created him

THREE ACTORS – WHICH SHOW?

Use these clues for the grid on the next page

ACROSS

1 Howard Hesseman, Robin Givens, Khrystyne Haje
8 Stephanie Zimbalist, Pierce Brosnan, Doris Roberts
11 George Peppard, Dirk Benedict, Dwight Schultz
13 John Forsythe, Linda Evans, Joan Collins
16 Robert Ulrich, Avery Brooks, Rob McLarty
17 Linda Lavin, Beth Howland, Vic Tayback
22 Dabney Coleman, Joanna Cassidy, Max Wright
23 Michael Gross, Meredith Baxter, Michael J. Fox
27 Scott Bakula, Dean Stockwell, Deborah Pratt
29 Craig T. Nelson, Jerry Van Dyke, Shelley Fabares
32 Dan Castellaneta, Julie Kavner, Nancy Cartwright
35 Mark Linn-Baker, Bronson Pinchot, Melanie Wilson
36 Bill Cosby, Phylicia Rashad, Malcolm-Jamal Warner
37 Tony Danza, Judith Light, Katherine Helmond
38 Soleil Moon Frye, George Gaynes, Cherie Johnson
39 Mel Harris, Peter Horton, Patricia Wettig

DOWN

1 John Ritter, Debrah Farentino, Felton Perry
2 Harry Morgan, Jamie Farr, Brandis Kemp
3 Brian Keith, Daniel Hugh Kelly, Mary Jackson
4 Christopher Hewett, Bob Uecker, Ilene Graff
5 Ricardo Montalban, Hervé Villechaize, Wendy Schaal
6 William Katt, Connie Selleca, Robert Culp
7 Pernell Roberts, Brian Stokes Mitchell, Charles Siebert
9 Leslie Nielsen, Alan North, Ed Williams
10 Ed Begley, Jr., Howie Mandel, Denzel Washington
12 Michael Landon, Victor French, James Troesh
14 Angela Lansbury, William Windom, Ron Masak
15 Nell Carter, Kari Michaelsen, Dolph Sweet
18 Lee Majors, Heather Thomas, Douglas Barr
19 William Shatner, Heather Locklear, Adrian Zmed
20 Don Johnson, Phillip Michael Thomas, Edward James Olmos
21 Alan Thicke, Joanna Kerns, Tracey Gold
22 Linda Hamilton, Ron Perlman, Roy Dotrice
24 Andy Griffith, Nancy Stafford, Clarence Gilyard, Jr.
25 Fred Savage, Dan Lauria, Danica McKellar
26 Matt Frewer, Amanda Pays, Jeffrey Tambor
28 Richard Mulligan, Dinah Manoff, Park Overall
30 Dana Delaney, Marg Helgenberger, Michael Boatman
31 David Hasselhoff, Pamela Anderson, Yasmine Bleeth
33 Gavin MacLeod, Fred Grandy, Bernie Kopell
34 Richard Dean Anderson, Dana Elcar, Bruce McGill

THREE ACTORS – WHICH SHOW?

Use the clues on the previous page

Solution on page 115

GENERAL KNOWLEDGE 20

solution on page 115

ACROSS

1 This jam band was formed in 1983 by a group of students in Burlington, Vermont

5 George Bush was the acting president on July 13, 1985, while Reagan underwent surgery to remove polyps from his ______

6 Common name for the antidepressant Fluoxetine, first prescribed in 1986

9 AC/DC and The Clash both made their US TV debuts on this SNL-inspired show,

11 Teen actor who went up against Jason, Gremlins, Lost Boys, *and* the Fratellis

12 Featured in "Fast Times at Ridgemont High," the Car's "Moving in ______"

13 The main character of the book featured in "The Neverending Story"

15 Professional wrestler who often appeared in Cyndi Lauper videos, Captain Lou ______

17 1982 parody of Gilbert and Sullivan starring Kristy McNichol, "The ______ Movie"

18 F. Murray Abraham plays this Italian composer in "Amadeus"

19 Spin-off of "Spenser for Hire" starring Avery Brooks, "A Man Called ______"

DOWN

1 This band released "A Momentary Lapse of Reason" in 1987, their first album without co-founder Roger Waters

2 Steve Vai plays the Devil's lead guitarist in this 1986 Ralph Macchio film

3 In 1986, this singer bought an interest in a Tennessee amusement park.

4 Operation Just Cause was the codename for the 1989 US invasion of this country

7 Launched in 1980, this bubble gum comes in a chewing tobacco-like pouch

8 In 1987, a farm in Sussex was found to have had the first case of Bovine Spongiform Encephalopathy, more commonly known as "______ disease",

10 Harrison Ford must find his kidnapped wife in Paris in this 1988 mystery thriller

14 Implanted in 1982, the world's first permanent artificial heart was named after its inventor, Robert ______.

16 Groundbreaking 1988 animated film taking place in Neo-Tokyo

ACTION MOVIES 3

solution on page 116

ACROSS

1 This 1980 martial arts action comedy was Jackie Chan's first attempt to break into the American movie market

2 Chuck Norris and Louis Gossett Jr. star as wisecracking treasure hunters

4 A New York police officer has a very eventful Christmas holiday in L.A.

7 Clint Eastwood and his orangutan are back for more bare-knuckle fighting

9 Classic 1981 actioner with globetrotting archaeologist Indiana Jones

12 A trucker, enlisted to help save his buddy's fiance, finds himself in a supernatural battle beneath Chinatown

14 Richard Chamberlain stars as adventurer Allan Quartermain in this 1985 film

16 A group of Soviet/Cuban guerrillas try to start a ruckus in Florida, only to meet Chuck Norris

17 Gene Hackman plays a retired Colonel who leads a group looking for POWs

18 Rutger Hauer plays a blind, sword fighting Vietnam veteran

19 Martial artist Leroy Green goes on a journey to find "The Glow." SHO-NUFF!

DOWN

1 Timothy Dalton took over the role of James Bond in this 1987 film

2 Michael Keaton steals Jack Nicholson's balloons.

5 This 1983 Dirty Harry film is the source of the catchphrase "Go ahead, make my day."

6 A group of Louisiana National Guard members piss off the wrong Cajuns

8 Bond film in which Roger Moore infamously disguises himself as a clown

10 Lee Marvin and Mark Hamill star in this 1980 film set during World War 2

11 A retired Special Forces colonel has to rescue his kidnapped daughter, played by Alyssa Milano

12 This early Jean-Claude Van Damme film involves an underground, full-contact martial arts tournament

13 Arnold Schwarzenegger plays a former FBI agent turned small-town sheriff who infiltrates the Chicago mafia

15 A hotshot naval aviator goes to train at the United States Navy's Fighter Weapons School, does fairly well.

SONG LYRICS – NAME THE SONG

ACROSS

2 A singer in a smokey room. A smell of wine and cheap perfume.

6 Earth below us, drifting, falling. Floating weightless, coming home….

7 Everybody's talking all this stuff about me. Why don't they just let me live?

11 And a hundred lonely housewives clutch empty milk bottles to their hearts

13 In violent times you shouldn't have to sell your soul.

18 Your friends don't dance and if they don't dance, well they're no friends of mine

20 Don't crack up. Bend your brain. See both sides. Throw off your mental chains

21 I wish I was in Tijuana eating barbequed iguana

23 Little voice inside my head said "Don't look back, you can never look back."

27 So needless to say, I'm odds and ends but I'll be stumblin' away slowly learnin' that life is okay

28 You own the money; you control the witness

29 You're saying that my love ain't real. Just look at my face, these tears ain't drying.

31 You don't know how desperate I've become and it looks like I'm losing the fight

32 Another night slowly closes in, and I feel so lonely

33 When we hear the voices sing, the book of love will open up and let us in

34 If you wanna find all the cops they're hanging out in the donut shops

35 Hey Ducky – let me stick the 7-inch in the computer

36 Cause when you say you will, it always means you won't.

38 Still gotta make a decision: leave tonight, or live and die this way

39 The time has come to say fair's fair. To pay the rent, to pay our share.

40 Does she walk? Does she talk? Does she come complete?

41 Life is a moment in space, when the dream is gone it's a lonelier place

42 A million lights are dancing and there you are, a shooting star

DOWN

1 Some boys take a beautiful girl and hide her away from the rest of the world

3 Though his mind is not for rent, don't put him down as arrogant

4 Your heart sweats, your teeth grind. Another kiss, and you'll be mine

5 "I'm happy, hope you're happy too. I've loved all I've needed, love. Sordid details following."

8 Rising up, straight to the top. Had the guts, got the glory

9 Pushing the day into the nighttime; somewhere between the two, we start to see

10 Too many shadows, whispering voices, faces on posters, too many choices.

12 I'm a man without conviction. I'm a man who doesn't know how to sell a contradiction.

14 An invisible man sleepin' in your bed. Ow, who you gonna call?

15 I don't wanna touch you too much baby, 'cause makin' love to you might drive me crazy

16 Subtle innuendos follow, there must be something inside.

17 Through the hourglass, I saw you. In time, you slipped away.

19 Her hair reminds me of a warm safe place where as a child I'd hide

22 He lives in his own heaven collects it to go from the 7-Eleven

23 You said you didn't need her. You told her goodbye. You sacrificed a good love to satisfy your pride

24 All I keep thinking about is her in my arms and I won't feel the same until she is mine

25 I'm never gonna dance again, guilty feet have got no rhythm

26 I'm your knight in shining armor and I love you. You have made me what I am, and I am yours.

30 Show me round your fruit cage 'cause I will be your honey bee

37 Tonight, make it magnificent. Tonight, make it tonight. Your hair is beautiful. Oh, tonight

SONG LYRICS – NAME THE SONG

Lyrics to the left – fill in the name of the song on this page!

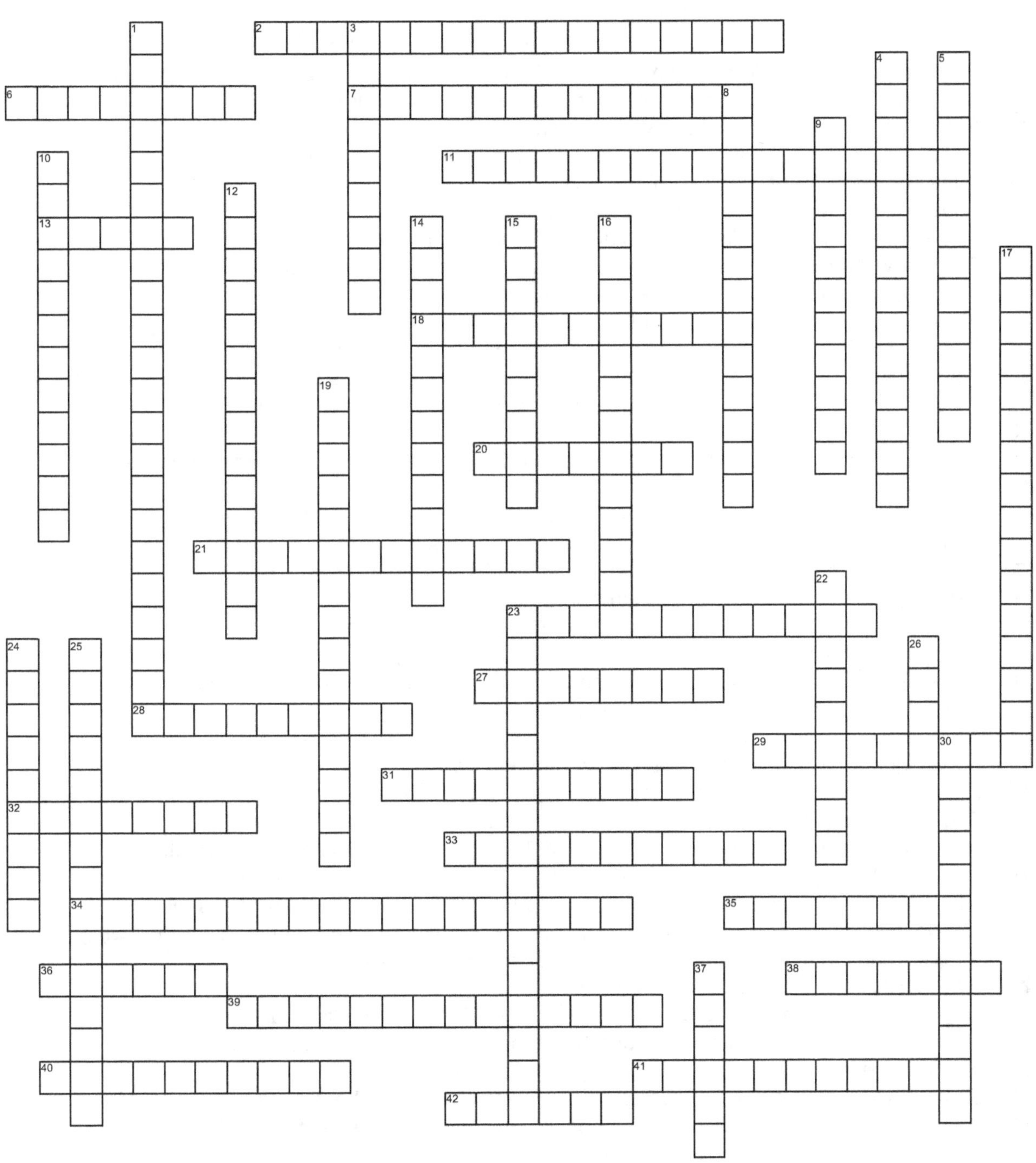

solution on page 116

SONG LYRICS - WHO SANG IT?

ACROSS

2 Life is a moment in space, when the dream is gone it's a lonelier place
4 He lives in his own heaven collects it to go from the 7-Eleven
7 I'm your knight in shining armor and I love you. You have made me what I am, and I am yours.
10 Tonight, make it magnificent. Tonight, make it tonight. Your hair is beautiful. Oh, tonight
13 The time has come to say fair's fair. To pay the rent, to pay our share.
17 Another night slowly closes in, and I feel so lonely
18 And a hundred lonely housewives clutch empty milk bottles to their hearts
24 Does she walk? Does she talk? Does she come complete?
27 Cause when you say you will, it always means you won't.
30 So needless to say, I'm odds and ends but I'll be stumblin' away slowly learnin' that life is okay
33 Too many shadows, whispering voices, faces on posters, too many choices.
34 In violent times you shouldn't have to sell your soul.
35 A singer in a smokey room. A smell of wine and cheap perfume.
37 Everybody's talking all this stuff about me. Why don't they just let me live?
38 You said you didn't need her. You told her goodbye. You sacrificed a good love to satisfy your pride
39 When we hear the voices sing, the book of love will open up and let us in
40 You own the money; you control the witness
41 I don't wanna touch you too much baby, 'cause makin' love to you might drive me crazy

DOWN

1 You don't know how desperate I've become and it looks like I'm losing the fight
3 If you wanna find all the cops they're hanging out in the donut shops
5 Hey Ducky – let me stick the 7-inch in the computer
6 Earth below us, drifting, falling. Floating weightless, coming home….
8 Though his mind is not for rent, don't put him down as arrogant
9 Pushing the day into the nighttime; somewhere between the two, we start to see
10 Through the hourglass, I saw you. In time, you slipped away.
11 An invisible man sleepin' in your bed. Ow, who you gonna call?
12 Subtle innuendos follow, there must be something inside.
14 I'm never gonna dance again, guilty feet have got no rhythm
15 Show me round your fruit cage 'cause I will be your honey bee
16 I'm a man without conviction. I'm a man who doesn't know how to sell a contradiction.
19 Your friends don't dance and if they don't dance, well they're no friends of mine
20 All I keep thinking about is her in my arms and I won't feel the same until she is mine
21 "I'm happy, hope you're happy too. I've loved all I've needed, love. Sordid details following."
22 A million lights are dancing and there you are, a shooting star
23 Her hair reminds me of a warm safe place where as a child I'd hide
25 Don't crack up. Bend your brain. See both sides. Throw off you mental chains
26 I wish I was in Tijuana eating barbequed iguana
28 Rising up, straight to the top. Had the guts, got the glory
29 Some boys take a beautiful girl and hide her away from the rest of the world
31 Your heart sweats, your teeth grind. Another kiss, and you'll be mine
32 Still gotta make a decision: leave tonight, or live and die this way
36 Little voice inside my head said "Don't look back, you can never look back."

SONG LYRICS WHO SANG IT?

Fill in the artists that sang the songs listed on the left!

solution on page 116

GENERAL KNOWLEDGE 21

solution on page 116

ACROSS

1 Harold Faltermeyer's 1984 hit song from the soundtrack to "Beverly Hills Cop"

4 This future Oscar winner got his start in "The Goonies" and "Indiana Jones and the Temple of Doom"

5 A forest boy must rescue a fair princess and the last of the unicorns in this 1985 film

6 Tears for Fears' second studio album, "Songs from the Big ______"

8 The name of the fortune teller machine that appears in "Big"

9 Name of the artificial Intelligence that almost starts WW3 in 1983's "WarGames"

13 Israeli actor and singer who played Dr. Hans Zarkov in "Flash Gordon"

15 Believe it or not, this band's "Pretty Hate Machine" was released in 1989.

16 1980 Robert Redford drama, based on a 1967 Arkansas prison scandal

17 1986 Dennis Quaid / Ellen Barkin thriller, "The Big ____"

18 1985's "Silver Bullet" was based on the Stephen King story "Cycle of the ______"

DOWN

2 In "Stand By Me," Gordie tells a story about David Hogan, AKA ________

3 Guitarist for Ozzy Osbourne, killed in a 1982 plane accident

7 Name of the demigod heard by Dana Barrett from inside her refrigerator in "Ghostbusters"

10 1986 sports drama about a small-town Indiana high school basketball team.

11 Billy Crystal SNL character, with the catchphrase "You Look Marvelous"

12 The secret phrase that causes cast members of "You Can't Do That on Television" to get slimed.

14 Look. I know I used this clue in an earlier puzzle, but I just want to reinforce how awful it was to see James Bond dressed up as a damn circus clown in this movie.

GENERAL KNOWLEDGE 22

solution on page 117

ACROSS

1 In 1984, Michael Jackson was burned while filming a commercial for this product

4 In 1988, this "hardest working man in show business" made police in two states work extra hard while pursuing him

6 This series of period comedies starring Rowan Atkinson aired from 1983 to 1989

7 Character played by Arnold Schwarzenegger in 1987's "Predator"

8 Syndicated music TV show that featured hosts Marilyn McCoo, Andy Gibb, and others

14 In "Heathers," this word was underlined by J.D. in Heather Duke's copy of "Moby Dick"

17 Actor who played Ted Theodore Logan

18 1981 film in which Ed Harris plays the king of a group of motorcycle riding medieval reenactors.

DOWN

2 Disney's second Florida park, opened in 1982.

3 An eight-year war began when this country invaded Iraq in 1980.

5 Launched in 1983, this tiny candy was sold in boxes that contained two separate flavor compartments

6 At 14 years old, this actress/model was the youngest cover girl of Vogue ever, a distinction she still has.

9 In "Escape From New York," Isaac Hayes played the _____ of New York

10 Nickname of Charlie's best friend in "Fright Night"

11 Financier know for developing the junk bond market, Michael _______

12 In 1988, Jamaica debuted this Winter Olympic team

13 Villainous family name from "The Goonies"

15 In "The Karate Kid," Daniel LaRusso goes to the Halloween dance dressed as one of these so he can "be invisible"

16 Huey Lewis and the News' 1983 album, where they really came into their own, commercially and artistically

ACTORS IN A MOVIE 3

ACROSS

2 Cher, Nicholas Cage, Olympia Dukakis
3 Gene Hackman, Willem Dafoe, Frances McDormand
6 Danny Devito, Bette Midler, Judge Reinhold
7 Andrew McCarthy, Kim Cattrall, Estelle Getty
9 Sally Field, Shirley MacLaine, Olympia Dukakis
10 Patrick Swayze, Jennifer Grey, C. Thomas Howell
11 Ed Harris, Mary Elizabeth Mastrantonio, Michael Biehn
16 Jack Nicholson, Shelley Duvall, Scatman Crothers
18 Daniel Day-Lewis, Brenda Fricker, Kirsten Sheridan
22 Robert De Niro, Jeremy Irons, Aidan Quinn
24 Jennifer Beals, Michael Nouri, Lilia Skala
30 Prince Markiee Dee, Kool Rock-Ski, Buff Love, Ralph Bellamy
33 Steve Guttenberg, Ally Sheedy, Fisher Stevens
34 Anthony Michael Hall, Ilan Mitchell-Smith, Kelly LeBrock
36 Arnold Schwarzenegger, James Earl Jones, Max von Sydow
37 Annabeth Gish, Lili Taylor, Julia Roberts
39 John Belushi, Dan Aykroyd, Cathy Moriarty
40 Dan Monahan, Wyatt Knight, Kim Cattrall
41 Josh Brolin, Sean Astin, Ke Huy Quan
42 Melanie Griffith, Harrison Ford, Sigourney Weaver
43 Elisabeth Shue, Keith Coogan, Anthony Rapp

DOWN

1 Michael Keaton, Griffin Dunne, Marilu Henner
4 Alex Baldwin, Geena Davis, Michael Keaton
5 Billy Crystal, Gregory Hines, Joe Pantoliano
8 Chevy Chase, Geena Davis, Joe Don Baker
12 Jeff Bridges, David Warner, Bruce Boxleitner
13 Adrienne Barbeau, Jamie Lee Curtis, John Houseman
14 Meryl Streep, Robert Redford, Klaus Maria Brandauer
15 Dennis Quaid, Louis Gossett, Jr., Brion James
17 Michael Douglas, Charlie Sheen, Darryl Hannah
18 Matt Dillon, Chris Makepeace, Joan Cusack
19 Steve Martin, John Candy, Edie McClurg
20 Michael J. Fox, Christopher Lloyd, Crispin Glover
21 Peter Billingsly, Darren McGavin, Melinda Dillon
23 Chevy Chase, Goldie Hawn, Charles Grodin
25 Dudley Moore, Eddie Murphy, Kate Capshaw
26 Eddie Murphy, Dan Aykroyd, Jamie Lee Curtis
27 Michael Douglas, Glenn Close, Anne Archer
28 Lea Thompson, Tim Robbins, Jeffrey Jones
29 Jeff Bridges, Kris Kristofferson, Christopher Walken
31 Holly Hunter, Albert Brooks, William Hurt
32 John Candy, Dan Aykroyd, Annette Bening
35 Jonathan Pryce, Ian Holm, Robert DeNiro
38 Charlie Sheen, Tom Berenger, Willem Dafoe

ACTORS IN A MOVIE 3

solution on page 117

ONE HIT WONDERS 2

Name the artists of these classics…

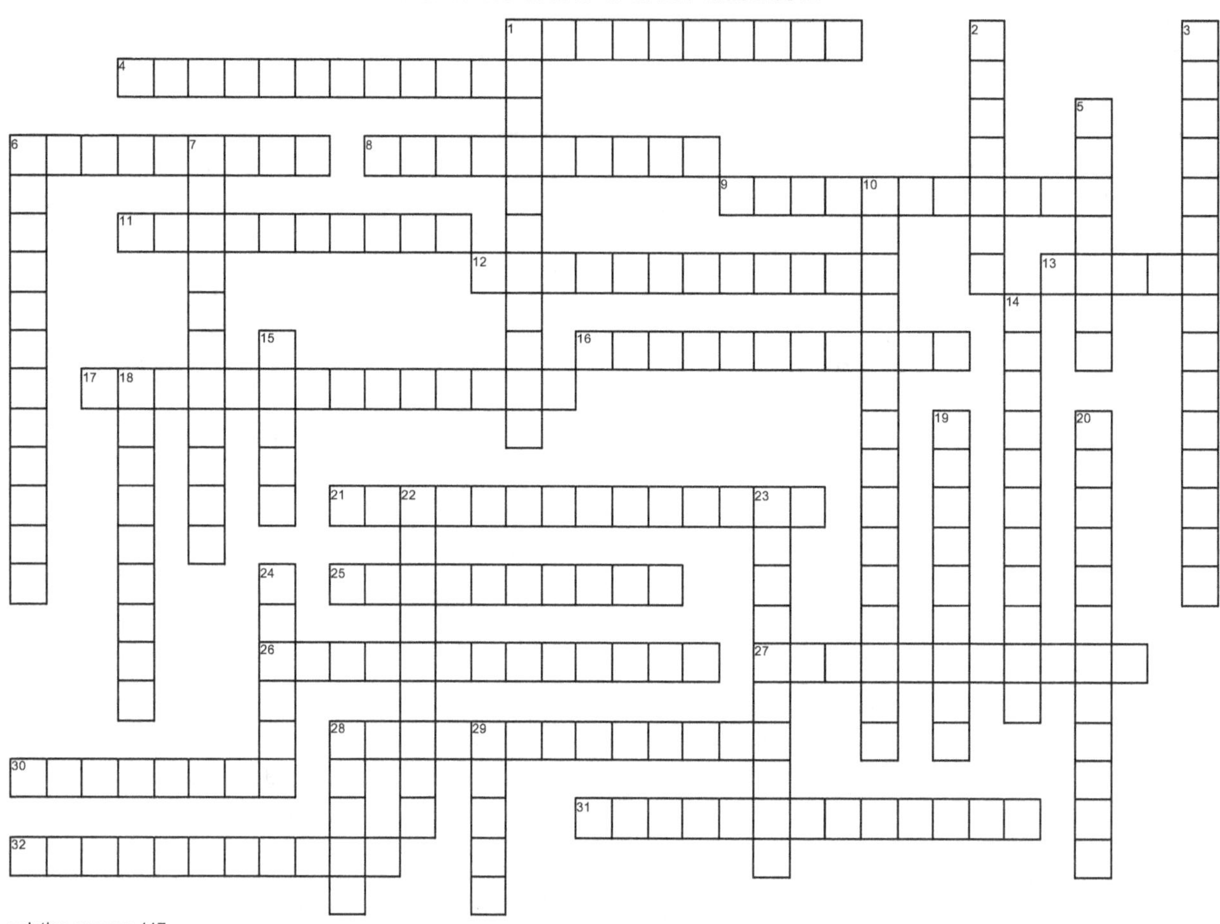

solution on page 117

<table>
<tr><td colspan="2">ACROSS</td><td colspan="2">DOWN</td></tr>
<tr><td>1</td><td>Voices Carry</td><td>1</td><td>Your Love</td></tr>
<tr><td>4</td><td>The Lady in Red</td><td>2</td><td>I Can't Wait</td></tr>
<tr><td>6</td><td>Tarzan Boy</td><td>3</td><td>We Don't Have to Take Our Clothes Off</td></tr>
<tr><td>8</td><td>Heartbeat</td><td>5</td><td>Toy Soldiers</td></tr>
<tr><td>9</td><td>Baby I Love Your Way / Freebird Medley</td><td>6</td><td>Waiting for a Star to Fall</td></tr>
<tr><td>11</td><td>All I Need</td><td>7</td><td>No Myth</td></tr>
<tr><td>12</td><td>Der Kommissar</td><td>10</td><td>Some Like It Hot</td></tr>
<tr><td>13</td><td>Edge of a Broken Heart</td><td>14</td><td>I Wanna Be a Cowboy</td></tr>
<tr><td>16</td><td>Beds are Burning</td><td>15</td><td>Rock Me Amadeus</td></tr>
<tr><td>17</td><td>19</td><td>18</td><td>Obsession</td></tr>
<tr><td>21</td><td>Major Tom</td><td>19</td><td>Theme to Miami Vice</td></tr>
<tr><td>25</td><td>The Promise</td><td>20</td><td>Black Velvet</td></tr>
<tr><td>26</td><td>Break My Stride</td><td>22</td><td>Under the Milky Way</td></tr>
<tr><td>27</td><td>Party All the Time</td><td>23</td><td>Wouldn't It Be Good</td></tr>
<tr><td>28</td><td>In My House</td><td>24</td><td>The Neverending Story</td></tr>
<tr><td>30</td><td>Somebody's Watching Me</td><td>28</td><td>Pump Up the Volume</td></tr>
<tr><td>31</td><td>Tenderness</td><td>29</td><td>Supersonic</td></tr>
<tr><td>32</td><td>Buffalo Stance</td><td></td><td></td></tr>
</table>

GENERAL KNOWLEDGE 23

solution on page 117

ACROSS

2 Released in 1979, this Gary Numan song is considered one of the first new wave hits

6 This Tim Conway character appeared in numerous 'straight to tape' films where he would play different sports (badly)

9 The National Academy of Recording Arts and Sciences revoked this band's Grammy for 1989's "Best New Artist."

10 This lead singer for AC/DC passed away in 1980. The coroner classified it as "death by misadventure."

13 Anwar Sadat, president of this country, was assassinated on October 6, 1981

14 Kenneth Branagh made his directorial debut in this 1989 Shakespeare adaptation

15 This band provided the soundtrack to the film "Highlander"

17 "The Final _______," 1980 film about a modern aircraft carrier that travels through time to 1941 Pearl Harbor

18 Bolstered by hits "These Dreams" and "What About Love," this band's self-titled 1985 album went to #1

19 This Greenpeace vessel was sunk by the French in 1985.

DOWN

1 1980 John Travolta film, "______ Cowboy"

3 He played Bill S. Preston Esq. in "Bill and Ted's Excellent Adventure"

4 1983 film, definitely the only adaptation of Hamlet featuring a mouse in a beer bottle.

5 Cartoon villain from "Press Your Luck"

7 Loose biopic about the Village People, "Can't Stop the ____"

8 She was the first female artist with an album to debut at #1 on the Billboard 200

11 The lead character in "Night of the Comet" is obsessed with maintaining all the high scores on this 1981 Atari video game

12 This Swiss electronic music band's song "Oh Yeah" was prominently featured in "Ferris Bueller's Day Off" and "The Secret of My Success"

16 This beloved video game character was actually the villain in "Donkey Kong Jr."

COMEDY MOVIES 3

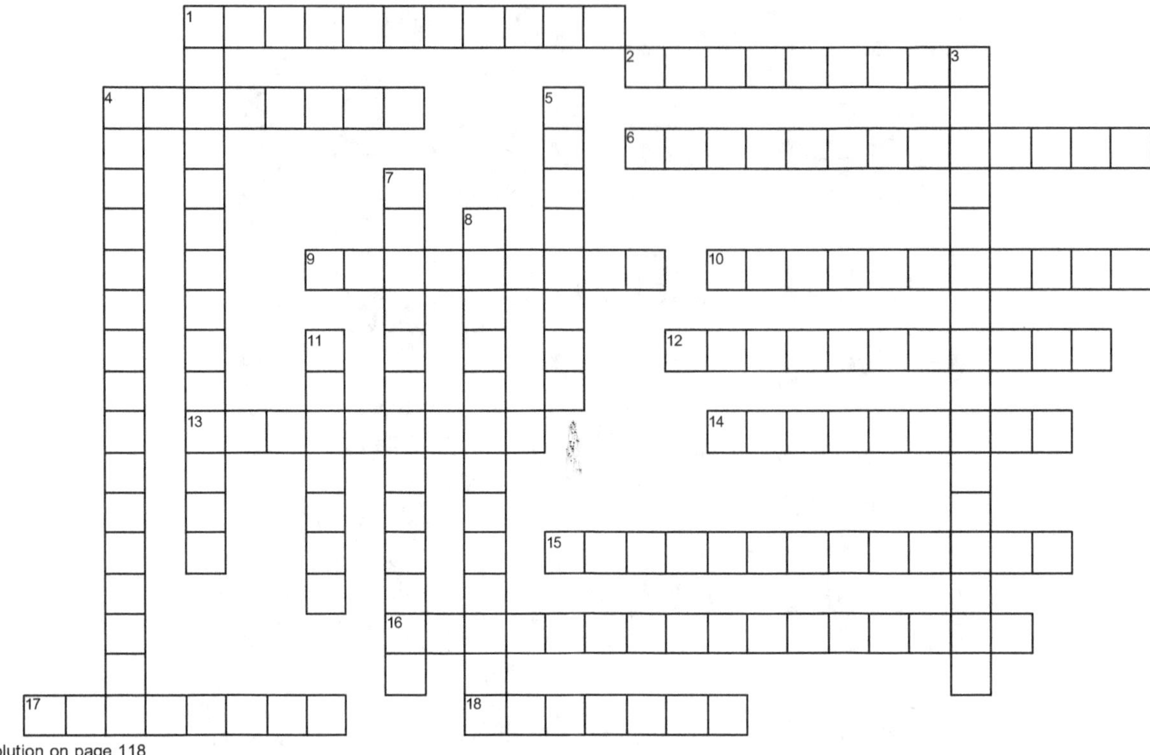

solution on page 118

ACROSS

1 Three silent film stars are mistaken for their film characters by the people of a small Mexican village.

2 A US rock singer helps the French Resistance rescue a scientist from East Germany

4 A washed-up pilot must take control when the flight crew gets food poisoning

6 A pair of yuppies buy a Winnebago and decide to "drop out;" it doesn't go well

9 A carefree bachelor is recruited to babysit his nieces and nephew

10 A couple buy a house that needs a little work. Did I say, "a little?" That was a lie.

12 Two low-level government workers are trained to be spies; don't realize they're actually expendable decoys

13 A carpenter rescues a socialite with amnesia; convinces her that she's actually his wife. Pretty sure that's illegal as hell.

14 A man is set up with a girl, is told not to let her drink. She does, and hijinks ensue

15 Two rich old men make a bet on "nature vs nurture," switching the lives of a wealthy commodities trader and a street hustler

16 A crew of oddballs engage in an illegal cross-country race

17 A girl hooks up with the new kid in town, who wants to kill the popular students

18 Parody/homage of a long-running police drama in which a pair of mismatched cops must fight a cult called P.A.G.A.N.

DOWN

1 A neat policeman must team with a slobbery French Mastiff to solve a crime

3 Five high school kids spend a Saturday in detention; learn stuff about themselves.

4 An unwitting barrister is drawn into a group of double-crossing jewel thieves

5 Bored neighbors begin to suspect that the new folks in town are devil worshippers

7 On the eve of his wedding, a man is thrown a wild party by his friends.

8 A high school student's list of problems includes drag racers, getting dumped, a paperboy, and raisins. *You like raisins*

11 Two unmotivated New Yorkers decide on a whim to join the Army. They're sent to Italy *but let's be honest the movie kind of peters out after the graduation scene*

FEVER DREAMS

I'm still not sure I didn't just make these movies up.

solution on page 118

ACROSS

3 Two brothers open a vegetarian restaurant as a front for them to kill women so they can resurrect the goddess Sheetar

4 Teenagers are attacked by a mall's robotic security force

9 A guy has to compete with his computer for the affections of his cellist neighbor

10 Nazis unleash a supernatural monster in a castle and wait who the hell is the good guy here?

13 Two brothers vie for the attention of a woman. Oh, and one's deformed and lives in a basket. Almost forgot that part.

15 Space herpes. This movie has space herpes in it. *Yes, I said "space herpes"*

18 Two guys set up a brothel in the morgue.

19 Two inept American detectives work a murder scene for Scotland Yard. But the fever dream part is because of "wookalars"

20 Gary Coleman lives in a train station locker. *You read that correctly.*

21 Beachgoers are sucked under the sand and eaten by a monster.

DOWN

1 A man answers a pay phone, and learns that the bombs drop in 70 minutes

2 A white law student pretends to be black so he can get a scholarship and *oh boy…*

5 There's Chevy Chase and Nazis and Little People. Just what every 80s movie needed

6 Elliot from "E.T." has an imaginary spy friend and spy-stuff happens

7 Chevy Chase (again!) dies and comes back as Benji. Yes, Benji the dog.

8 Scott Baio gets telekinetic powers, immediately starts being an asshole

11 A liquor store sells cheap booze to winos, not knowing it causes people to melt.

12 A teen thinks his parents are in a cult. Nope, they're just a different species that…like melts into each other.

14 Andy Kauffman and Bernadette Peters are robots in love.

16 Jackie Gleason buys Richard Pryor for his spoiled brat kid. That seems wrong.

17 That same kid from 16-down gets sued by the IRS for his fertilizer company.

3 MOVIES, 1 ACTOR 2

Use the grid on the next page. You're doing great, by the way.

ACROSS

2 Vampire's Kiss, Peggy Sue Got Married, Raising Arizona
4 Down and Out in Beverly Hills, 48 Hrs., Three Fugitives
9 E.T. the Extra-Terrestrial, Firestarter, Irreconcilable Differences
11 Diner, Leviathan, C.H.U.D.
13 The Secret of My Success, Light of Day, Teen Wolf
14 Spaceballs, To Be or Not to Be, History of the World: Part I
17 Raising Arizona, Broadcast News, Always
18 Coming to America, Conan the Barbarian, Return of the Jedi
19 Punchline, Nothing in Common, Dragnet
20 The Delta Force, Missing in Action, Firewalker
22 All the Right Moves, Losin' It, Legend
24 Silverado, No Way Out, Bull Durham
27 Rumble Fish, Drugstore Cowboy, Target
28 Excalibur, Krull, Next of Kin
29 Stand By Me, The Lost Boys, The Goonies
32 The Adventures of Baron Munchausen, The Best of Times, Moscow on the Hudson
35 Lethal Weapon, The Color Purple, Witness
36 Dangerous Liaisons, Fatal Attraction, The World According to Garp
38 Blind Fury, The Hitcher, Blade Runner
40 A Nightmare on Elm Street, Platoon, Private Resort
42 Videodrome, Cop, Salvador
43 The Star Chamber, A Chorus Line, The War of the Roses
44 Ladyhawke, WarGames, Max Dugan Returns
45 Summer Rental, Armed and Dangerous, Brewster's Millions

DOWN

1 The Elephant Man, 1984, Heaven's Gate
3 Mississippi Burning, Hoosiers, Superman II
5 Wall Street, Platoon, Ferris Bueller's Day Off
6 Top Gun, Willow, Real Genius
7 Blind Date, Sunset, Die Hard
8 The Fly, Silverado, The Adventures of Buckaroo Banzai Across the Eighth Dimension
10 The Year of Living Dangerously, Mad Max Beyond Thunderdome, The River
12 D.O.A., Innerspace, When Harry Met Sally…
15 Running Scared, Throw Momma from the Train, The Princess Bride
16 Beetlejuice, Married to the Mob, Talk Radio
21 My Beautiful Laundrette, My Left Foot, The Unbearable Lightness of Being
23 Sixteen Candles, Pretty in Pink, The Pick-Up Artist
25 Pale Rider, Tightrope, Pink Cadillac
26 City Heat, Paternity, The Best Little Whorehouse in Texas
30 Back to School, Less Than Zero, Weird Science
31 Murphy's Law, Assassination, Death Wish II
33 Hannah and Her Sisters, Deathtrap, Jaws IV: The Revenge
34 Funny Farm, Modern Problems, Deal of the Century
37 Red Dawn, Dirty Dancing, Roadhouse
39 Pretty in Pink, Hiding Out, Superman IV: The Quest for Peace
41 Moonstruck, The Witches of Eastwick, Mask

3 MOVIES, 1 ACTOR 2

solution on page 118

HORROR MOVIES 3

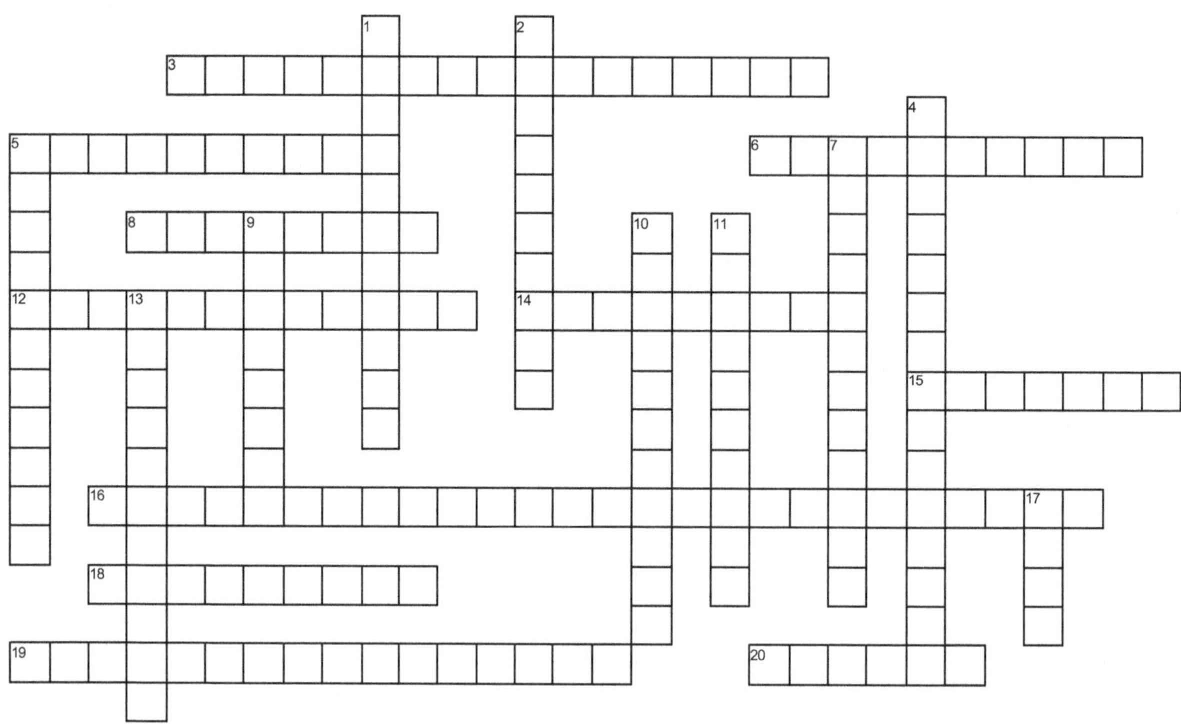

solution on page 118

ACROSS

3 This 1984 documentary, hosted by Donald Pleasence and Nancy Allen, compiled clips from dozens of horror films,

5 A struggling writer gets a winter gig as the caretaker of a hotel. Doesn't help him write.

6 A young woman is terrorized by the spirit of an axe murderer after using a Ouija board

8 Residents of a New Zealand village are harvested by an intergalactic fast-food joint.

12 A literary critic thinks he's been bitten by a vampire; goes completely mental

14 Speaking of vampires, a race of space vampires comes to earth and chaos ensues

15 Michael Caine loses his hand, then his mind

16 Townspeople must fight aliens, balloon animals, when the wrong circus lands in town.

18 Susan Sarandon is a sleep researcher who gets involved with a vampire couple (David Bowie and Catherine Deneuve)

19 Karen Black and Louise Fletcher star in this remake of a 1953 film where aliens land, take over people with mind control,

20 A French anthropologist gets involved with a group of demonic Inuit trickster spirits. It doesn't go particularly well for him.

DOWN

1 A teen enlists the help of a television host to fight the vampire next-door

2 A serial killer performs a voodoo ritual to transfer his soul to a kid's doll.

4 A group of boys learn the answer to the question, "Does the wolfman have nards?"

5 "Oh, it's a book bound in human flesh. Hey, let's see what it has to say."

7 Martin Sheen is a psychologist who finds himself mixed up with a Hispanic cult

9 Baron Frankenstein creates a woman for his monster; ends up falling in love with her instead.

10 A group of teens think it would be cool to spend the night in a sketchy carnival's dark ride. You know that's a bad idea, right?

11 Four elderly men share a dark murderous secret, and now that secret is coming back to haunt them.

13 A group of kids accidentally kill a small-town boy. The boy's father has a local witch summon a vengeance demon. *Parents, talk to your kids about vengeance demons.*

17 He was a good dog. Until he wasn't.

SCI-FI MOVIES 3

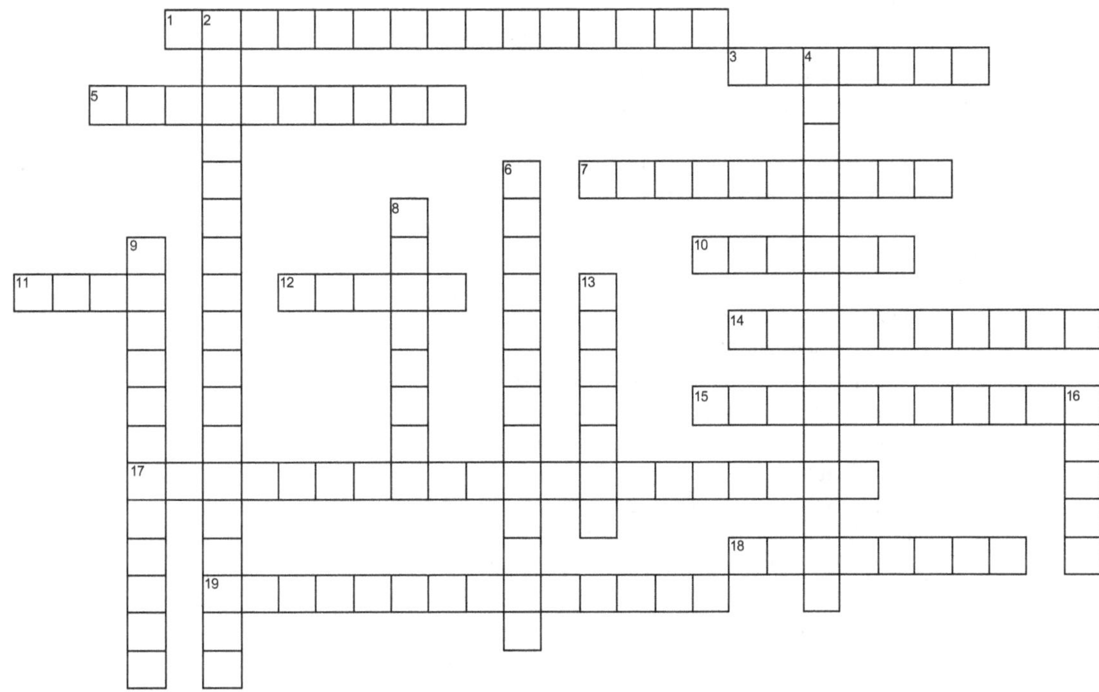

solution on page 118

ACROSS

1 Paul Le Mat and Nancy Allen star in this 1983 homage to sci-fi films of the 1950s

3 Tom Selleck is a police officer assigned to stop Gene Simmons' murderous robots

5 A test pilot is miniaturized and accidentally injected in an unsuspecting grocery clerk

7 Based on a DC comic, a scientist becomes a marsh bound monster who gets exposed to chemicals when his lab is sabotaged

10 A group of elderly folks sneak into a swimming pool and are exposed to extraterrestrial powers.

11 Frank Herbert's epic tale of the fall of House Atreides is told in this film

12 Jeff Goldblum and Cyndi Lauper are psychics hired to find a lost Incan city.

14 A disturbed girl is taken to a sanitarium because she's obsessed with some weird land where there's a yellow road.

15 A nerdy social misfit – played by Kathy Ireland – falls down a hole and ends up in Atlantis.

17 A boy disappears for eight years; is found unaged. He also now has a psychic connection with a recently discovered alien spacecraft.

18 Tensions mount after an alien presence inadvertently sinks a U.S. submarine near the Cayman Trough

19 Two gelflings must restore balance to the world by restoring a powerful crystal

DOWN

2 Everyone said Alex was wasting his time playing that damn video game. Well, guess who saved us from the Ko-Dan Armada.

4 Most life on Earth is wiped out when it passes through a comet's tail. Two Valley Girls do what they must to maintain order.

6 An angel in Berlin chooses to become mortal after falling in love

8 There's a new dessert on the market. No calories! It's Sweet! It's Filling! It's alive! Wait, say that last one again?

9 A smarty-pants kid puts a computer chip into a dead girl's head. Now she's back, and lethal with a basketball.

10 Jeff Bridges is an alien who takes the form of a widow's husband and enlists her help to get to a rescue site.

16 In futuristic Neo Tokyo, a biker gets telekinetic powers, and chooses to use them for evil rather than good. Then it gets weird. Then it gets weirder.

THREE CHARACTERS IN A MOVIE 2

ACROSS

2 Ariel, Sebastian, Flounder
5 Mr. Creosote, Death, Man with Bendy Arms
7 C. D. Bales, Dixie, Roxanne Kowalski
14 Vincent, Carmen, Eddie Felton
16 Jed Eckert, Erica Mason, Col. Andy Tanner
17 David Lightman, John McKittrick, Stephen Falken
18 Mrs. White, Wadsworth, Mr. Boddy
19 Seymour Krelborn, Audrey, Mr. Mushnik
27 Alex Rogan, Centauri, Grig
28 Sarah, Jareth, Hoggle
29 Jack Torrance, Dick Hallorann, Lloyd the Bartender
34 Dusty Bottoms, Lucky Day, Ned Nederlander
36 Virgil "Bud" Brigman, Lindsey Brigman, Hiram Coffey
37 Irwin Fletcher, Gail Stanwyk, Larry
38 Alex Murphy, Clarence Boddicker, Anne Lewis
40 John McClane, Hans Gruber, Al Powell
41 Garry Wallace, Wyatt Donnelly, Lisa
42 Jake Taylor, Ricky Vaughn, Roger Dorn
43 Freddy Benson, Lawrence Jamieson, Janet Colgate
45 Crash Davis, Annie Savoy, Ebby Calvin "Nuke" Laloosh

DOWN

1 Kevin Flynn, Alan Bradley, Lora Baines
3 Harry Angel, Louis Cyphre, Epiphany Proudfoot
4 Frank Cross, Claire Phillips, and *Mary Lou Retton as Tiny Tim*
5 Sam Weber, Sarah Cooper, Alex (the dead guy)
6 Martin Riggs, Roger Murtaugh, Mr. Joshua
8 John Winger, Russell Ziskey, Sergeant Hulka
9 Julia Cotton, Frank Cotton, The Hell Priest / Pinhead
10 William H. Bonney, Jose Chavez y Chavez, Pat Garrett
11 Dottie, Francis Buxton, Large Marge
12 Andie Walsh, Blane McDonagh, Duckie Dale
13 Isabelle de Merteuil, Sebastien de Valmont, Marie de Tourvel
15 Ponyboy Curtis, Johnny Cade, Dallas Winston
20 Jenny Fields, Roberta Muldoon, Ellen James
21 Arthur, Merlin, Morgana Le Fay
22 Alan Swann, Benjy Stone, K.C. Downing
23 King Osric, Valeria, Thulsa Doom
24 Samantha Baker, Farmer Ted, Jake Ryan
25 Perseus, Andromeda, Ammon
26 Joan Wilder, Jack Colton, Ralph
30 Archie Leach, Wanda Gershwitz, Otto West
31 Robert Gould Shaw, Private Silas Trip, Sergeant Major John Rawlins
32 Ray Kinsella, Terence Mann, Shoeless Joe Jackson
33 Mrs. Brisby, The Great Owl, Nicodemus
35 San Enersibm Edgar Frog, Star
39 Clark W, Griswold, Ellen Griswold, Roy Walley
44 George Newman, Pamela Finklestein, Stanley Spadowski

THREE CHARACTERS IN A MOVIE 2

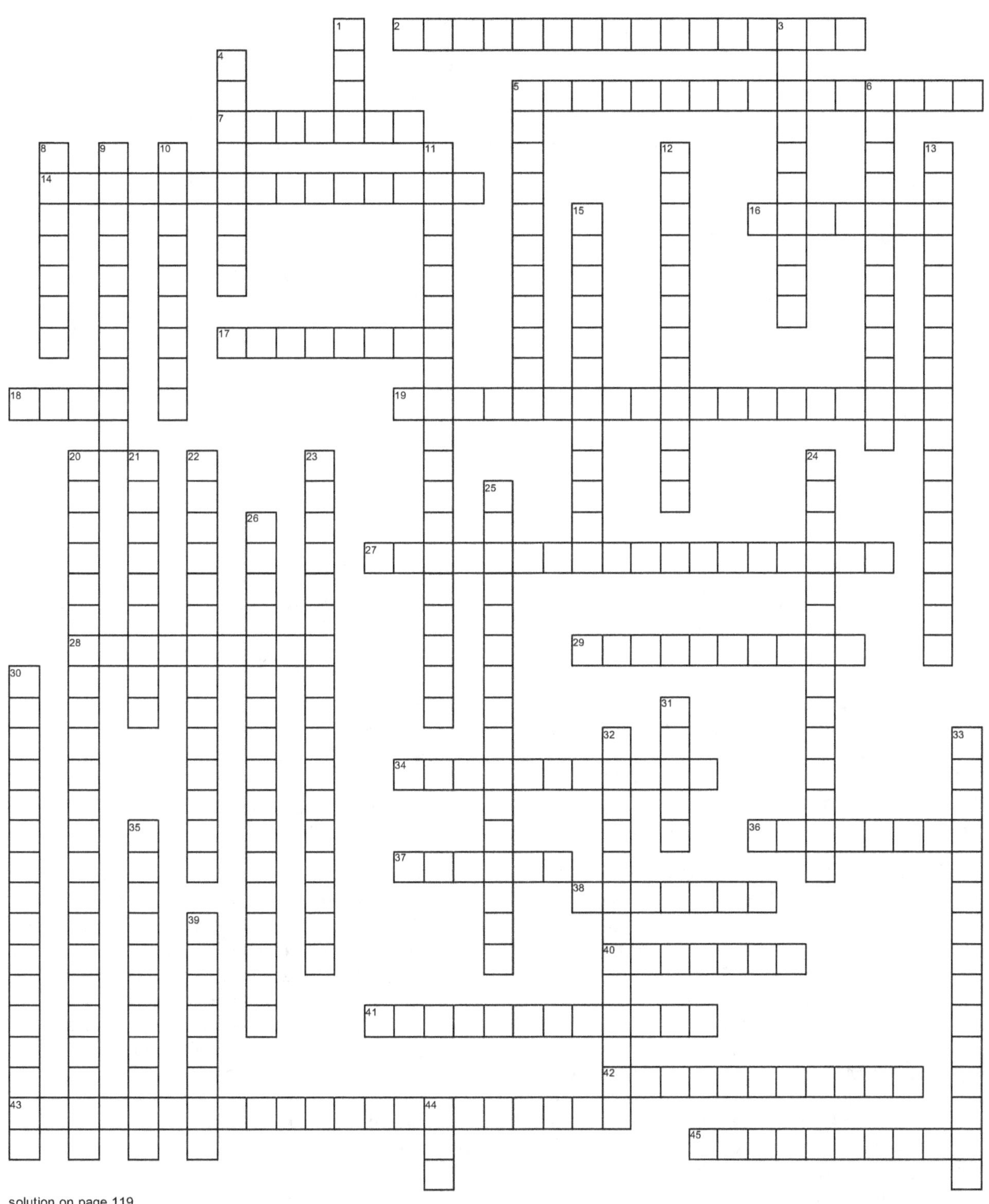

solution on page 119

TEEN MOVIES

solution on page 119

<u>ACROSS</u>

1 William Ragsdale is a teen who thinks his next-door neighbor is a vampire.

5 Winona Ryder is a teen who hooks up with the new psycho at school; popular girls start dropping

10 Corey Haim is a teen who joins the football team to impress a girl.

15 Jennifer Grey is a teen who someone dares to try put in a corner.

17 Molly Ringwald is a teen whose family forgets her birthday

19 A group of teens go to detention.

20 Corey Feldman is a teen who swaps consciousnesses with Jason Robards.

21 A group of teens have to spend their vacation in remedial English

22 Kevin Bacon is a teen who moves to a town with a law against dancing.

<u>DOWN</u>

2 Ralph Macchio is a teen who learns how to defend himself against bullies

3 Deborah Foreman is a teen who falls for a Hollywood punk.

4 Corey Haim is a teen whose brother gets involved with the wrong bloodsucking crowd.

6 Patrick Swayze leads a group of teens who must fight the Russians in Colorado

7 Two teens decide to use their computer to create a "perfect woman."

8 John Cusack is a teen who falls for the school valedictorian

9 C. Thomas Howell is a teen who must run when his fellow greaser kills a Soc.

10 Corey Haim (yes, again) is a teen who fails his driving license test, goes on driving adventures nevertheless.

11 Molly Ringwald is a teen who must choose between her best friend and a preppy boy

12 Patrick Dempsey is a teen who mows a lot of lawns, also rents a girlfriend.

13 John Cusack is a teen whose girlfriend dumps him for the ski team captain.

14 Tom Cruise is a teen who turns his house into a brothel to pay for Porsche repairs.

16 Michael J. Fox is a teen who plays basketball, learns about a dark family secret. *More relatable than 14-down.*

18 Andrew McCarthy is a teen who unknowingly sleeps with his roommate's mother. Yes, that's problematic.

SOLUTIONS

PAGE 5
ACROSS

3	BORN IN THE USA
5	YEAR
8	DELOREAN
9	SEA WORLD
11	PLAID
12	JAPAN
16	THE DAY AFTER
17	POST-IT NOTES
19	KILL
20	JOURNEY

DOWN

1	JIMMY HOFFA
2	RED
3	BOB
4	HERO
6	FEZZIK
7	BAND-AID
8	DOUBLE DARE
10	DEPECHE MODE
13	CLAPPER
14	FARM-AID
15	KRULL
18	FLO

PAGE 9
ACROSS

1	BLOW OUT
7	HUGO
8	DIVIDE
10	FIREFOX
12	PLATOON
15	LOS ANGELES
18	MCFERRIN
19	A VIEW TO A KILL
20	REDFORD
21	COLUMBIA

DOWN

2	LOOKER
3	THIEF
4	BRIAN
5	REAGAN
6	HUMUNGUS
9	FOX
11	IT TAKES TWO
13	CLAN
14	FERRARO
16	MEMOIRS
17	J. J. FAD

PAGE 6
ACROSS

6	POLTERGEIST
8	THE SURE THING
10	NEAR DARK
15	FIELD OF DREAMS
17	SILKWOOD
20	TOP GUN
21	WHEN HARRY MET SALLY
23	FOOTLOOSE
25	DEAD POETS SOCIETY
26	DRESSED TO KILL
28	A NIGHTMARE ON ELM STREET
33	THE LOST BOYS
35	MASTERS OF THE UNIVERSE
39	BODY HEAT
40	RISKY BUSINESS
41	LADYHAWKE
42	THE NATURAL
43	DRIVING MISS DAISY

DOWN

1	TOOTSIE
2	ST ELMOS FIRE
3	GREMLINS
4	TEEN WOLF
5	BEVERLY HILLS COP
7	TERMS OF ENDEARMENT
9	REDS
11	BLUE VELVET
12	ROBOCOP
13	RAINMAN
14	STIR CRAZY
16	GOOD MORNING VIETNAM
18	DRUGSTORE COWBOY
19	BACK TO SCHOOL
22	LEGEND
24	LETHAL WEAPON
27	FIRESTARTER
29	A ROOM WITH A VIEW
30	THE UNTOUCHABLES
31	NO HOLDS BARRED
32	SOPHIES CHOICE
34	DIRTY DANCING
36	RAGING BULL
37	DIE HARD
38	STRIPES

PAGE 8
ACROSS

1	SUMMER SCHOOL
6	BEETLEJUICE
7	RUTHLESS PEOPLE
8	MR. MOM
9	HANKY PANKY
13	DIRTY ROTTEN SCOUNDRELS
14	GHOSTBUSTERS
17	STRANGE BREW
18	LOOK WHO'S TALKING
19	REVENGE OF THE NERDS

DOWN

1	SIXTEEN CANDLES
2	ONE CRAZY SUMMER
3	VOLUNTEERS
4	TIN MEN
5	GUNG HO
6	BACK TO SCHOOL
10	CADDYSHACK
11	BULL DURHAM
12	BILOXI BLUES
15	TWINS
16	BIG

PAGE 10
ACROSS

2	DYNASTY
4	BEAUTY AND THE BEAST
7	MURDER, SHE WROTE
9	MATLOCK
10	KNOTS LANDING
13	TRAPPER JOHN M.D.
15	THE EQUALIZER
16	DALLAS
17	HIGHWAY TO HEAVEN
18	FALCON CREST
19	LIFE GOES ON
20	IN THE HEAT OF THE NIGHT

DOWN

1	L.A. LAW
3	THE FALL GUY
5	SIMON AND SIMON
6	ST. ELSEWHERE
7	MACGYVER
8	HILL STREET BLUES
11	MOONLIGHTING
12	CHINA BEACH
14	MIAMI VICE

PAGE 11
ACROSS

4	THE HUMAN LEAGUE
7	THE POLICE
8	JOE JACKSON
11	BLONDIE
12	EURYTHMICS
13	THE GO-GOS
14	THE CHURCH
15	ERASURE
16	THE CARS
18	PET SHOP BOYS
20	MISSING PERSONS
22	TEARS FOR FEARS
25	BANANARAMA
27	DURAN DURAN
31	THOMPSON TWINS
32	ALPHAVILLE

DOWN

1	YAHOO
2	TALKING HEADS
3	THE PSYCHEDELIC FURS
4	THE SMITHS
5	NEW ORDER
6	DEPECHE MODE
8	JOY DIVISION
9	A FLOCK OF SEAGULLS
10	DEVO
17	CROWDED HOUSE
19	THOMAS DOLBY
21	SPANDAU BALLET
22	TIL TUESDAY
23	ROXY MUSIC
24	BERLIN
25	SQUEEZE
28	R.E.M.
29	THE CURE
30	INXS

PAGE 12
ACROSS

1	PORKCHOP
6	BONO
7	BUTTERCUP
9	MODERN
13	ELLEN FOLEY
15	ACID
17	SARAJEVO
18	DAS BOOT
20	EASTWICK
21	CHILL

DOWN

2	CONDORMAN
3	BLUES
4	SQUARE PEGS
5	REPO MAN
8	CONFLICT
10	SHOWTIME
11	LAKE PLACID
12	POLYESTER
14	LAGOON
16	RAOUL
19	ASH

PAGE 14
ACROSS

2	SPY HUNTER
4	FROGGER
6	JOUST
8	OUTRUN
9	TRACK AND FIELD
10	CONTRA
12	CENTIPEDE
14	BURGERTIME
18	MILLIPEDE
20	GALAGA
21	DRAGON'S LAIR
22	ROBOTRON

DOWN

1	GHOST N GOBLINS
2	STREET FIGHTER
3	MISSILE COMMAND
5	GAUNTLET
7	DONKEY KONG
11	DEFENDER
13	DIG-DUG
15	RAMPAGE
16	PAPERBOY
17	Q*BERT
19	PAC-MAN

PAGE 13
ACROSS

6	SOME GREAT REWARD
8	DISINTEGRATION
10	THRILLER
11	SCARECROW
15	SYNCHRONICITY
17	GRACELAND
21	HOUNDS OF LOVE
25	SHE'S SO UNUSUAL
26	THE RIVER
27	PRIVATE DANCER
29	ELIMINATOR
30	PURPLE RAIN
31	LIKE A PRAYER
32	THE NYLON CURTAIN

DOWN

1	HYSTERIA
2	CAN'T SLOW DOWN
3	SO
4	METAL HEALTH
5	BROTHERS IN ARMS
7	AND JUSTICE FOR ALL
9	ESCAPE
12	NEW JERSEY
13	FULL MOON FEVER
14	KICK
16	INVISIBLE TOUCH
18	LICENSED TO ILL
19	LOOK SHARP
20	MAKE IT BIG
21	HI-INFIDELITY
22	BACK IN BLACK
23	PUMP
24	FAITH
28	CONTROL

PAGE 15
ACROSS

1 GYMKATA
4 NEXT OF KIN
8 FIREFOX
12 ACTION JACKSON
14 RUNAWAY TRAIN
15 WANTED DEAD OR ALIVE
16 NIGHTHAWKS
17 KICKBOXER
18 RENT-A-COP
19 ALIENS
20 NEVER SAY NEVER AGAIN

DOWN

2 THE RUNNING MAN
3 RED SONJA
5 MISSING IN ACTION
6 COBRA
7 THE DEAD POOL
9 RED SCORPION
10 THE KARATE KID
11 SHOOT TO KILL
13 ROADHOUSE

PAGE 20
ACROSS

2 YOUNGBLOOD
4 ORDINARY
5 MASK
8 REPLICANT
9 STRIPES
10 VAN HALEN
11 DIP
14 PERSEUS
15 ZOD
17 JEOPARDY
18 WATCHER
19 GHOST STORY
20 MS-DOS

DOWN

1 GOOSE
3 GORBACHEV
5 MEL BROOKS
6 KYLIE MINOGUE
7 HOT SPACE
8 ROADHOUSE
12 OCTOPUS
13 CRAZY
16 HICKS

PAGE 16
ACROSS

2 CALL ME
4 FOOTLOOSE
6 BIG TIME
14 YOU MAY BE RIGHT
17 UNDER PRESSURE
18 VOICES CARRY
22 HOW SOON IS NOW?
26 BLUE MONDAY
27 PURPLE RAIN
29 THE WAITING
31 TRUE COLORS
33 CARS
34 PRIVATE DANCER
35 I RAN
37 BURNING DOWN THE HOUSE
38 THE GREATEST LOVE OF ALL

DOWN

1 ETERNAL FLAME
3 MAGIC
5 HEAD OVER HEELS
7 HUNGRY LIKE THE WOLF
8 PRETTY IN PINK
9 EYE IN THE SKY
10 DESIRE
11 SYNCHRONICITY II
12 FAITH
13 THRILLER
15 PHYSICAL
16 TENDERNESS
19 JUST LIKE HEAVEN
20 ALL OUT OF LOVE
21 THE WAY IT IS
23 STEPPIN' OUT
24 NEED YOU TONIGHT
25 BORN IN THE U.S.A.
28 DEBASER
30 JUMP
32 STRANGELOVE
36 HELLO

PAGE 18
ACROSS

1 BILLY JOEL
9 JOE JACKSON
10 BRUCE HORNSBY
14 AIR SUPPLY
17 WHITNEY HOUSTON
18 THE CURE
19 BLONDIE
20 THE CARS
22 VAN HALEN
23 DEPECHE MODE
24 A FLOCK OF SEAGULLS
25 TEARS FOR FEARS
29 KENNY LOGGINS
31 BRUCE SPRINGSTEEN
32 TOM PETTY
34 THE ALAN PARSONS PROJECT
35 'TIL TUESDAY
36 TINA TURNER
37 NEW ORDER

DOWN

2 LIONEL RICHIE
3 THE PIXIES
4 QUEEN
5 GENERAL PUBLIC
6 DURAN DURAN
7 CYNDI LAUPER
8 OLIVIA NEWTON JOHN
11 TALKING HEADS
12 MICHAEL JACKSON
13 PRINCE
15 THE PSYCHEDELIC FURS
16 GARY NUMAN
21 TAYLOR DAYNE
25 THE SMITHS
26 THE POLICE
27 GEORGE MICHAEL
28 THE BANGLES
30 PETER GABRIEL
33 INXS

PAGE 21
ACROSS
2 FULL HOUSE
5 WEBSTER
7 TOO CLOSE FOR COMFORT
9 THE FACTS OF LIFE
11 NEWHART
15 HEAD OF THE CLASS
16 SEINFELD
17 A DIFFERENT WORLD
18 VALERIE
19 NIGHT COURT
20 CHEERS
21 GROWING PAINS
22 MY TWO DADS

1 BENSON
3 ALF
4 KATE AND ALLIE
5 WHO'S THE BOSS
6 BOSOM BUDDIES
8 THE GOLDEN GIRLS
10 SILVER SPOONS
12 THE COSBY SHOW
13 MAMA'S FAMILY
14 AMEN

PAGE 22
ACROSS
3 THE STEPFATHER
5 CAT'S EYE
7 POLTERGEIST
10 HOUSE
13 MAXIMUM OVERDRIVE
14 THE HOWLING
15 MOTEL HELL
16 CRITTERS
17 NEAR DARK
18 THE FLY
19 THE GATE

1 VAMP
2 CREEPSHOW
4 MY BLOODY VALENTINE
5 CHRSTINE
6 NIGHT OF THE CREEPS
8 THE HITCHER
9 SILVER BULLET
10 HELLRAISER
11 DEAD RINGERS
12 THE LOST BOYS

PAGE 23
ACROSS
3 BEETLEJUICE
5 GUMMI BEARS
8 VOLTRON
10 THUNDARR THE BARBARIAN
14 THE SMURFS
15 RAINBOW BRITE
17 ROBOTECH
18 THUNDERCATS
19 MY LITTLE PONY
20 TEENAGE MUTANT NINJA TURTLES

1 DEFENDERS OF THE EARTH
2 DUCKTALES
4 INSPECTOR GADGET
6 BRAVESTARR
7 POUND PUPPIES
9 CARE BEARS
10 TRANSFORMERS
11 MUPPET BABIES
12 G. I. JOE
13 JEM
16 SHE-RA

PAGE 26
ACROSS
2 CADDYSHACK
4 FLASH GORDON
6 LABYRINTH
8 VALLEY GIRL
9 SHORT CIRCUIT
19 OVER THE TOP
22 THE LOST BOYS
23 ROCKY III
24 THE WOMAN IN RED
25 SAY ANYTHING
DOWN
1 VACATION
3 DO THE RIGHT THING
5 XANADU
7 DIRTY DANCING
10 HONEYSUCKLE ROSE
11 REAL GENIUS
12 STREETS OF FIRE
13 FOOTLOOSE
14 AGAINST ALL ODDS
15 HEAVY METAL
16 BETTER OFF DEAD
17 VISION QUEST
18 THE KARATE KID
20 PRETTY IN PINK
21 WORKING GIRL

----------------PAGE 24----------------
ACROSS
3 MOONLIGHTING
8 IN THE HEAT OF THE NIGHT
9 MURPHY BROWN
10 VALERIE
11 BENSON
12 BOSOM BUDDIES
14 THE FACTS OF LIFE
16 SILVER SPOONS
19 CHARLES IN CHARGE
20 HART TO HART
24 ROSEANNE
26 WISEGUY
28 THE GOLDEN GIRLS
30 DALLAS
31 THAT'S INCREDIBLE
32 WEBSTER

DOWN
1 DOOGIE HOWSER, M.D.
2 HILL STREET BLUES
4 KNOT'S LANDING
5 PEE WEE'S PLAYHOUSE
6 THE EQUALIZER
7 MAMA'S FAMILY
13 DESIGNING WOMEN
14 THE YOUNG ONES
15 SAVED BY THE BELL
17 NIGHT COURT
18 MARRIED WITH CHILDREN
19 CHEERS
21 ALF
22 A DIFFERENT WORLD
23 FAMILY MATTERS
25 AMEN
27 FULL HOUSE
29 NEWHART

PAGE 27
ACROSS

1 AIRPLANE!
5 STIR
6 MTV
7 A-HA
8 FAMILY MATTERS
11 EARTHQUAKE
12 THE FAR SIDE
15 JOHN LENNON
17 JANUARY
18 COBRA

DOWN

2 RAINMAN
3 GLOBE
4 MIRACLE
6 MEMBERS ONLY
9 LIBYA
10 EASTENDERS
13 VISITORS
16 AC/DC

PAGE 28
ACROSS

1 THE EMPIRE STRIKES BACK
10 MY SCIENCE PROJECT
11 HIGHLANDER
12 WILLOW
14 THE PRINCESS BRIDE
17 E.T. THE EXTRATERRESTRIAL
18 WARGAMES
19 THE TERMINATOR

DOWN

1 TIME BANDITS
2 ELECTRIC DREAMS
3 BLADE RUNNER
4 SHORT CIRCUIT
5 LOOKER
6 LABYRINTH
7 RETURN OF THE JEDI
8 THEY LIVE
9 HEAVY METAL
13 LADYHAWKE
15 REPO MAN
16 KRULL

PAGE 29
ACROSS

2 POLTERGEIST
4 GHOSTBUSTERS
7 SCARFACE
9 ROBOCOP
10 COCKTAIL
11 LABYRINTH
13 THE BLUES BROTHERS
14 WILLOW
17 REPO MAN
19 THEY LIVE
20 MEGAFORCE
21 AMADEUS
22 CLUE
23 WALL STREET
25 LA BAMBA
27 COBRA
28 FLETCH
29 HIGHLANDER
30 JAWS: THE REVENGE
31 AIRPLANE!

DOWN

1 COCOON
3 ROADHOUSE
5 TRON
6 BLADE RUNNER
8 A FISH CALLED WANDA
12 DIE HARD
15 THE THING
16 THE FLY
18 PLATOON
24 ALIENS
26 BIG

-----------------PAGE 30----------------

ACROSS

1 DEXY'S MIDNIGHT RUNNERS
4 BIG COUNTRY
6 A-HA
9 THE WAITRESSES
12 NAILS
13 JOHN PARR
14 YELLO
17 A FLOCK OF SEAGULLS
19 MADNESS
21 DEVO
22 THE VAPORS
23 SHANNON
24 TOM TOM CLUB
25 STACEY Q
26 KAJAGOOGOO
27 TONI BASIL
28 DEAD OR ALIVE
29 MODERN ENGLISH

DOWN

2 SOFT CELL
3 PRETTY POISON
4 BOW WOW WOW
5 THE BUGGLES
7 NENA
8 WALL OF VOODOO
10 THE WEATHERGIRLS
11 QUARTERFLASH
15 TOMMY TUTONE
16 EDDY GRANT
18 LIPPS, INC
20 GARY NUMAN

-----------------PAGE 31----------------

ACROSS

1 NEIL DIAMOND
6 LIVE AID
8 SHEPHERD
9 LONDON
12 CNN
13 TOUCH
16 IRON LADY
18 BANANARAMA
19 FIST
20 RUBIK'S CUBE

DOWN

2 NINTH
3 XANADU
4 ISLANDERS
5 METALLICA
7 ALLISON
10 NICE DREAMS
11 MONTANA
14 CMT
15 CRYSTAL
17 KARL

--------------------PAGE 32--------------------

	ACROSS			DOWN
3	WILLOW		1	FAST TIMES AT RIDGEMONT HIGH
9	BLADE RUNNER		2	MAXIMUM OVERDRIVE
14	BETTER OFF DEAD		4	WARGAMES
16	ALIENS		5	DIEHARD
17	STRIPES		6	PEE WEE'S BIG ADVENTURE
18	VACATION		7	THE KARATE KID
21	THIS IS SPINAL TAP		8	PREDATOR
24	GREMLINS		10	CADDYSHACK
27	PRETTY IN PINK		11	BODY HEAT
30	TIME BANDITS		12	THE PRINCESS BRIDE
31	WEIRD SCIENCE		13	REAL GENIUS
32	BATMAN		15	AIRPLANE!
34	STAND BY ME		19	THE BLUES BROTHERS
37	SUDDEN IMPACT		20	THE RUNNING MAN
38	ROXANNE		22	THE GOONIES
39	GHOSTBUSTERS		23	THREE AMIGOS
40	SPACEBALLS		25	TRADING PLACES
41	THE NAKED GUN		26	THE BREAKFAST CLUB
42	THE LOST BOYS			

--------------------PAGE 36--------------------

	ACROSS			DOWN
2	HILL STREET BLUES		1	CARLA
5	L.A. LAW		3	SCHNEIDER
7	JUDD HIRSCH		4	TAXI
9	FAMILY TIES		6	SHELLEY LONG
11	BARNEY MILLER		7	JIM
12	MAGNUM, P.I.		8	SHOGUN
16	SHARON GLES		10	LOU GRANT
18	HIGGINS		13	DUSTIN HOFFMAN
19	DANNY DEVITO		14	JOHN RITTER
22	THE GOLDEN GIRLS		15	PRIVATE BENJAMIN
25	THIRTYSOMETHING		17	MOONLIGHTING
26	CAROLE KANE		20	BETTY WHITE
27	BEA ARTHUR		21	ALAN ALDA
28	MASH		23	ESTELLE GETTY
31	BENSON		24	JANE CURTAIN
33	RUE MCCLANAHAN		29	PATTY DUKE
34	THE JEFFERSONS		30	THE COSBY SHOW
35	CAGNEY AND LACEY		32	ST. ELSEWHERE
36	JIM JONES		37	ED ASNER
38	CHEERS		40	DALLAS
39	TYNE DALY			
41	SOAP			
42	THE WONDER YEARS			

PAGE 34

	ACROSS
2	ATWOOD
6	CARD
9	RUSHDIE
10	HUBBARD
14	WALKER
15	ISHIGURO
17	KING
19	DELILLO
21	MAILER
22	KOONTZ
24	SAGAN
26	KEILLOR
27	CONROY
28	CLANCY
29	MARQUEZ
31	FOLLETT
32	WOLFE
33	TAN
34	MCMURTY

	DOWN
1	JAKES
2	ADAMS
3	DAHL
4	BUKOWSKI
5	PRATCHETT
7	LE CARRE
8	MORRISON
10	HARRIS
11	SUSKIND
12	HAWKING
13	TOOLE
15	IRVING
16	BARKER
18	GIBSON
20	LUDLUM
23	RICE
25	MCCARTHY
26	KUNDERAS
30	ECO

PAGE 35
ACROSS

3 BRONCO
4 DEAD OR ALIVE
8 SHRINKING
9 RAISINS
10 PEZ
12 SHANNON
13 BANANAS
15 EMMA THOMPSON
17 ELSA
19 NEW ORDER
20 RICHARD DAWSON

DOWN

1 MEMPHIS
2 SO FINE
3 BETAMAX
5 GLASNOST
6 DIPPIN' DOTS
7 JUST SAY NO
11 MADNESS
12 SCANNERS
14 O'CONNOR
16 DEVO
18 XTC

PAGE 43
ACROSS

1 LOVESICK
4 MAXELL
5 MR. BOOGEDY
6 WIRE
7 MR. T
10 ANDRE
14 LEAN ON ME
16 JUST DO IT
17 EUROPEAN
18 EL GUAPO
19 REESE

DOWN

2 SNORKS
3 STATES
4 MY BUDDY
6 WATCHMEN
7 MARVIN GAYE
8 DESMOND TUTU
9 THE SIMPSONS
11 BELLOQ
12 LOVERBOY
13 STALLONE
15 RAGTIME

PAGE 38
ACROSS

3 EMPIRE OF THE SUN
5 MAJOR LEAGUE
7 THE EVIL DEAD
11 BODY HEAT
15 BIG TOP PEE WEE
18 WILDCATS
22 RETURN TO OZ
24 THE WORLD ACCORDING TO GARP
25 SATISFACTION
26 MATEWAN
27 SOPHIE'S CHOICE
28 STAND BY ME

DOWN

1 POPEYE
2 CUTTING CLASS
4 MYSTIC PIZZA
6 HE KNOWS YOU'RE ALONE
7 TEEN WOLF TOO
8 LUCAS
9 WITHNAIL AND I
10 GOING OVERBOARD
11 BMX BANDITS
12 ENDLESS LOVE
13 MAX DUGAN RETURNS
14 TAPS
16 BLOOD SIMPLE
17 DIE HARD
19 THE GOONIES
20 BLIND DATE
21 WARGAMES
23 TOOTSIE

PAGE 39
ACROSS

3 OVER THE TOP
4 SHOCK TREATMENT
7 MIKE TYSON
10 TOTO
12 GATE
13 FRANCES
14 STAR TREK
17 SEOUL
18 TITANIC
19 FAME

DOWN

1 CUJO
2 MOONWALK
4 SAINT HELENS
5 MARS BLACKMON
6 FRANK SINATRA
8 SIRACHA
9 NUDE
11 TED
15 BRUCE
16 ROSE

PAGE 42
ACROSS

1 MICKEY GILLEY
3 EDDIE RABBIT
6 ALABAMA
7 WILLIE NELSON
9 CLINT BLACK
11 MERLE HAGGARD
13 JOHN CONLEE
14 RONNIE MILSAP
18 EARL THOMAS CONLEY
20 GEORGE STRAIT
21 THE JUDDS
22 JANIE FRICKE
23 KENNY ROGERS
24 BARBARA MANDRELL
25 DON WILLIAMS
26 RICKY SKAGGS
27 WAYLON JENNINGS

DOWN

2 CRYSTAL GAYLE
4 DAN SEALS
5 GARY MORRIS
8 CONWAY TWITTY
10 GEORGE JONES
12 DOLLY PARTON
15 JOHN ANDERSON
16 LEE GREENWOOD
17 RANDY TRAVIS
19 CHARLEY PRIDE

PAGE 40
ACROSS

3	RAINMAN
5	AMADEUS
6	WILLIAM HURT
12	SISSY SPACEK
18	DANIEL DAY LEWIS
19	CHER
22	THE LAST EMPEROR
25	PLATOON
30	GANDHI
31	GERALDINE PAGE
32	MARLEE MATLIN
35	OLIVER STONE
38	CHARIOTS OF FIRE
39	JESSICA LANGE
40	GEENA DAVIS
41	BEN KINGSLEY
42	DON AMECHE
43	PAUL NEWMAN
44	DENZEL WASHINGTON

DOWN

1	BARRY LEVINSON
2	SALLY FIELD
4	MICHAEL CAINE
7	RICHARD ATTENBOROUGH
8	SHIRLEY MACLAINE
9	KATHARINE HEPBURN
10	LINDA HUNT
11	ORDINARY PEOPLE
13	DRIVING MISS DAISY
14	DUSTIN HOFFMAN
15	MICHAEL DOUGLAS
16	JAMES L. BROOKS
17	MILOS FORMAN
20	WARREN BEATTY
21	JOHN GIELGUD
23	SYDNEY POLLACK
24	ROBERT DUVALL
26	HENRY FONDA
27	ROBERT REDFORD
28	KEVIN KLINE
29	JESSICA TANDY
32	MERYL STREEP
33	SEAN CONNERY
34	MICHAEL CAINE
35	OUT OF AFRICA
36	JODIE FOSTER
37	ROBERT DENIRO

PAGE 44
ACROSS

3	THE KARATE KID
5	THE THING
7	TOP SECRET!
9	THE COLOR PURPLE
13	RE-ANIMATOR
16	DO THE RIGHT THING
18	REAL GENIUS
21	THE PRINCESS BRIDE
22	SUMMER SCHOOL
23	TIME BANDITS
25	CHILDS PLAY
27	HIGHLANDER
29	HEATHERS
31	RETURN TO OZ
32	BETTER OFF DEAD
34	ESCAPE FROM NEW YORK
37	UNCLE BUCK
38	PREDATOR
40	COMING TO AMERICA
41	MIDNIGHT RUN
42	PURPLE RAIN

DOWN

1	AIRPLANE
2	BIG TROUBLE IN LITTLE CHINA
4	THE ELEPHANT MAN
5	THE NAKED GUN
6	FLASH GORDON
8	VIDEODROME
10	CADDYSHACK
11	ALIENS
12	BLADE RUNNER
14	STRANGE BREW
15	THE NEVERENDING STORY
17	FRIGHT NIGHT
19	THE TERMINATOR
20	MANHUNTER
24	ROADHOUSE
26	SPACEBALLS
28	THE MONSTER SQUAD
30	THE GOLDEN CHILD
33	THE RUNNING MAN
35	COMMANDO
36	SUPERGIRL
39	WILLOW

PAGE 46
ACROSS

1	PITBULL
3	EMMA STONE
5	TAYLOR SWIFT
10	LADY GAGA
11	ADAM DRIVER
13	CHRIS EVANS
17	EMILIA CLARKE
18	MICHAEL CERA
21	ADELE
22	AWKWAFINA
23	KAREN GILLAN

DOWN

2	BRITNEY SPEARS
3	EVA GREEN
4	LIN-MANUEL MIRANDA
6	RYAN GOSLING
7	JENNIFER HUDSON
8	NATALIE PORTMAN
9	KRISTEN BELL
12	CHRIS PINE
14	SHIA LABEOUF
15	BRIE LARSON
16	SARAH SNOOK
19	AVICII
20	DRAKE

PAGE 47
ACROSS

1	AGAINST ALL ODDS
4	CINEMAX
7	GEORGE BURNS
9	THE WALL
11	DAVID
14	F.A.O. SCHWARTZ
18	NOID
19	MIRROR

DOWN

2	TAB
3	STARCADE
4	CLAIRE
5	EIGHTH
6	MANIAC
8	BILL THE CAT
10	EXCALIBUR
12	DARLINGS
13	POPCORN
15	SHOWBIZ
16	THE TICK
17	ARMS

PAGE 48
ACROSS

1 DAN AYKROYD
5 HARRISON FORD
15 STEVE MARTIN
16 DEBRA WINGER
18 DEMI MOORE
19 WILLIAM HURT
20 CARRIE FISHER
25 JUDGE REINHOLD
31 SEAN PENN
33 SYLVESTER STALLONE
36 JACKIE CHAN
37 GEENA DAVIS
38 DENNIS HOPPER
39 RICHARD DREYFUSS
40 JOHN LITHGOW
41 CHRISTOPHER WALKEN
42 LAURENCE FISHBURNE

DOWN

2 KEANU REEVES
3 KIM BASINGER
4 WILFORD BRIMLEY
6 MICHAEL KEATON
7 SIGOURNEY WEAVER
8 GENE WILDER
9 ED HARRIS
10 TOM BERENGER
11 EDDIE MURPHY
12 SEAN CONNERY
13 SALLY FIELD
14 RICK MORANIS
17 KEVIN KLINE
21 ROBERT DENIRO
22 RICHARD PRYOR
23 WHOOPI GOLDBERG
24 JOHN CLEESE
25 JOHN MALKOVICH
26 DARYL HANNAH
27 DANNY DEVITO
28 MICKEY ROURKE
29 KURT RUSSELL
30 BILL MURRAY
31 SISSY SPACEK
32 MORGAN FREEMAN
34 KATHLEEN TURNER
35 JACK NICHOLSON
36 JEFF BRIDGES

PAGE 50
ACROSS

1 BLOCKBUSTER
4 WALLEY
6 QUIET RIOT
7 JOAN RIVERS
9 TRIVIAL PURSUIT
14 GLAIVE
16 TRAIN
17 KHAN
18 EDDIE
19 WALTER PAYTON

DOWN

1 BASQUIAT
2 CLUE
3 R.E.M.
5 LIES
8 AMADEUS
10 PROM NIGHT
11 RIPTIDE
12 TWINKIE
13 FUNKYTOWN
15 ARTHUR

PAGE 51
ACROSS

3 WHO FRAMED ROGER RABBIT
5 SCARFACE
7 EMPIRE OF THE SUN
9 FANDANGO
13 THE BLUES BROTHERS
14 ALWAYS
15 TWILIGHT ZONE
17 THE LAND BEFORE TIME
19 THE MONEY PIT
20 POLTERGEIST
21 THE GOONIES
22 E.T. THE EXTRA-TERRESTRIAL

DOWN

1 YOUNG SHERLOCK HOLMES
2 LAST CRUSADE
4 RAIDERS OF THE LOST ARK
6 AN AMERICAN TAIL
8 TEMPLE OF DOOM
10 BACK TO THE FUTURE
11 INNERSPACE
12 AMAZING STORIES
13 THE COLOR PURPLE
16 USED CARS
18 GREMLINS

------------------PAGE 52--------------------

ACROSS

3 NEW KIDS ON THE BLOCK
4 GEORGE MICHAEL
6 PRINCE
8 GUNS N ROSES
10 BRUCE SPRINGSTEEN
12 PHIL COLLINS
13 ANITA BAKER
14 METALLICA
17 DIRE STRAITS
19 TEARS FOR FEARS
21 VAN HALEN
23 BOBBY BROWN
24 JANET JACKSON
25 BEASTIE BOYS
26 CHICAGO
28 DEF LEPPARD
29 MADONNA
30 QUIET RIOT
31 THE POLICE
32 LIONEL RICHIE
33 MICHAEL JACKSON

DOWN

1 JOURNEY
2 GENESIS
5 CYNDI LAUPER
7 Z.Z. TOP
9 INXS
10 BON JOVI
11 PAUL SIMON
15 REO SPEEDWAGON
16 BILLY JOEL
18 PETER GABRIEL
20 FOREIGNER
22 AEROSMITH
27 AC/DC

PAGE 53
ACROSS
1 OLD TIMES
3 BIFF
6 SNAKE
7 ELEPHANT
10 WINGS
12 ROCKWELL
16 TAPS
17 LEAN CUISINE
18 OVALTINE
19 ANDREW
DOWN
2 THE BANGLES
3 BON JOVI
4 FUJI
5 CARBON COPY
8 CHERNOBYL
9 JUDAS PRIEST
11 CADDYSHACK
13 HAITI
14 POSTMAN
15 NEW COKE

PAGE 56
ACROSS
2 SCARFACE
7 THRILLER
10 CROSS
11 ENYA
12 JENNY
13 BAD BOYS
15 VICTORY
16 COWBOY
19 SIZZLE
20 COMMODORE
21 ZAGNUT
DOWN
1 BRAT
3 CUTTING CREW
4 FALKLANDS
5 GERTIE
6 VIGO
8 CAPRI-SUN
9 MOONLIGHTING
14 OVERLOOK
17 ENDOR
18 CHER

PAGE 57
ACROSS
6 C.H.U.D.
8 THE THING
9 TROLL
12 A NIGHTMARE ON ELM STREET
15 THE BLOB
17 PRINCE OF DARKNESS
18 THE DEAD ZONE
20 RE-ANIMATOR
21 GHOULIES
DOWN
1 THEY LIVE
2 CHILDREN OF THE CORN
3 TRICK OR TREAT
4 DAY OF THE DEAD
5 CAT PEOPLE
7 PET SEMATARY
10 BAD DREAMS
11 HELL NIGHT
13 SLEEPAWAY CAMP
14 RAWHEAD REX
16 BASKET CASE
19 ALIENS

--------------------PAGE 54--------------------
ACROSS
1 SPACECAMP
4 WHO'S THAT GIRL
8 RAISING ARIZONA
9 MY FAVORITE YEAR
10 VACATION
12 URBAN COWBOY
15 SCARFACE
16 SIXTEEN CANDLES
17 THE BREAKFAST CLUB
19 SPLASH
21 THE VERDICT
26 THE MONEY PIT
28 PRETTY IN PINK
29 BULL DURHAM
30 THE BURBS
31 BATMAN
33 USED CARS
35 SAY ANYTHING
36 RAIDERS OF THE LOST ARK
38 WARGAMES
39 PRIZZI'S HONOR
40 BIG
42 XANADU
43 AFTER HOURS
45 THE BIG CHILL
46 ORDINARY PEOPLE
47 WEEKEND AT BERNIE'S
48 LICENSE TO DRIVE
DOWN
2 POLICE ACADEMY
3 GLORY
5 THIS IS SPINAL TAP
6 ON GOLDEN POND
7 NIGHT SHIFT
11 DANGEROUS LIAISONS
13 OVERBOARD
14 NINE TO FIVE
18 FULL METAL JACKET
19 STAND BY ME
20 EXPLORERS
22 HOOSIERS
23 YOUNG GUNS
24 PRIVATE BENJAMIN
25 THE BLUES BROTHERS
27 DINER
32 MR. MOM
34 GHOSTBUSTERS
36 RHINESTONE
37 SPIES LIKE US
41 WITNESS
44 POPEYE

PAGE 60
ACROSS
1 BEASTIE BOYS
6 DE LA SOUL
8 KURTIS BLOW
11
12 FAT BOYS
14 SCHOOLY D
15 E.P.M.D.
16 ICE-T
20 DOUG E. FRESH
21 RAPPER'S DELIGHT
23 BIZ MARKIE
DOWN
2 EAZY-E
3 ULTRAMAGNETIC M.C.S
4 PUBLIC ENEMY
5 BIG DADDY KANE
7 L.L. COOL J
9 RUN-DM=C
10 WHODINI
13 ROXANNE
17 BODY ROCK
18 BRIDGE
19 MC LYTE
22 N.W.A.

----------------------PAGE 58----------------------

ACROSS

3	WILLIE NELSON
4	FAITH
8	BATMAN
9	USA FOR AFRICA
11	THRILLER
12	HIGHWAYMAN
13	DOUBLE FANTASY
15	BEACHES
16	PHYSICAL
18	KIM CARNES
19	BEAT IT
21	PHIL COLLINS
22	DOLLY PARTON
26	MICHAEL JACKSON
28	MIAMI VICE
29	BOBBY MCFERRIN
32	ANNE MURRAY
35	MEN AT WORK
36	LES MISERABLES
37	RICHARD PRYOR
38	CYNDI LAUPER
39	TINA TURNER
40	THE JUDDS

DOWN

1	ELVIRA
2	GRACELAND
5	HIGHER LOVE
6	CHRISTOPHER CROSS
7	AMY GRANT
10	SYNCHRONICITY
14	TRACY CHAPMAN
17	LIONEL RICHIE
20	THE JOSHUA TREE
23	JOHN WILLIAMS
24	SOMEWHERE OUT THERE
25	GOOD MORNING VIETNAM
27	LOVE
30	ROSANNA
31	EAT IT
33	RANDY TRAVIS
34	BONNIE RAITT

PAGE 61

ACROSS

1	EMPEROR
5	STARDUST
10	BULL TERRIER
11	EWOK
13	POTTS
16	AVIATORS
17	FANTASY
18	LISA
19	JAKE
20	SAL'S

DOWN

2	MASH
3	VICTORY
4	RUSSELL
6	AFRICA
7	SMALLPOX
8	TIME BANDITS
9	GIGOLO
12	JESSICA
13	POPEYE
14	THE FOG
15	CANADA

PAGE 62

ACROSS

5	ESCAPE FROM NEW YORK
10	ABOVE THE LAW
13	STREETS OF FIRE
15	CYBORG
16	RED DAWN
18	PREDATOR
19	RAMBO
20	BLUE THUNDER
21	THE TERMINATOR

DOWN

1	FIRST BLOOD
2	BEST OF THE BEST
3	IRON EAGLE
4	CONAN THE BARBARIAN
6	ROMANCING THE STONE
7	BLACK RAIN
8	HEARTBREAK RIDGE
9	TANGE AND CASH
11	THE KILLER
12	LETHAL WEAPON
14	HIGHLANDER
17	RED HEAT

PAGE 63

ACROSS

1	A CHRISTMAS STORY
5	TEACHERS
7	VICTOR/VICTORIA
10	MIDNIGHT RUN
11	EATING RAOUL
13	FERRIS BUELLER'S DAY OFF
15	EASY MONEY
18	MAJOR LEAGUE
20	PROTOCOL
21	PRIVATE BENJAMIN

DOWN

2	THIS IS SPINAL TAP
3	BEVERLY HILLS COP
4	POLICE ACADEMY
6	SPACEBALLS
8	THE NAKED GUN
9	TO BE OR NOT TO BE
12	YELLOWBEARD
14	FLETCH
16	ROXANNE
17	ALL OF ME
19	MOVING

PAGE 64

ACROSS

1	MADNESS
5	BRAINS
6	WINSLOW
8	VALDEZ
11	FLASH GORDON
15	SHIRLEY
16	CHRISTINE
17	BIZARRE
18	BILL WYMAN

DOWN

2	DINER
3	GRUBER
4	BIRD
6	WHAM
7	WHAT I AM
9	BERNIE
10	BOB MARLEY
12	JOHN HURT
13	NEWT
14	GAMEBOY

PAGE 65
ACROSS

2	WORKING GIRL
6	CHANCES ARE
8	THE SURE THING
9	COCKTAIL
11	BROADCAST NEWS
12	SAY ANYTHING
13	PRETTY IN PINK
14	TOOTSIE
16	DIRTY DANCING
17	ABOUT LAST NIGHT
18	ALWAYS
19	THE BLUE LAGOON
20	SOMEWHERE IN TIME

DOWN

1	THE PICK-UP ARTIST
2	WHEN HARRY MET SALLY
3	MANNEQUIN
4	ENDLESS LOVE
5	THE PRINCESS BRIDE
7	SPLASH
10	CAN'T BUY ME LOVE
15	ROXANNE

PAGE 68
ACROSS

5	MICHAEL JORDAN
6	DYNASTY
8	CHARIOTS
10	MINE
13	JACKET
14	CATS
15	TWINS
16	SEURAT
17	WINDOWS
19	NENA
20	SILKWOOD
21	LEVI STUBBS
22	SPECK

DOWN

1	HANDS
2	AIDS
3	BRUNO
4	PALM SPRINGS
7	THE COTTON CLUB
9	INTO THE WOODS
11	NOSTRADAMUS
12	WHITESNAKE
18	BLACK

-----------------------PAGE 66-----------------------
ACROSS

1	STUDEBAKER
8	SANTAYANA
10	DISNEYLAND
14	MARILYN MONROE
16	KHRUSHCHEV
18	ELVIS PRESLEY
24	EDSEL
28	BEATLEMANIA
29	SUGAR RAY
32	PANMUNJOM
33	CAMPANELLA
34	MALENKOV
35	WATERGATE
37	PAYOLA
41	MARCIANO
42	EINSTEIN
45	THALIDOMIDE
46	EICHMANN
47	ROSENBERGS
48	THE KING AND I
49	SALLY RIDE
50	RICHARD NIXON
52	CASTRO
53	KEROUAC
54	SYNGMAN RHEE
55	LIBERACE

DOWN

1	SUEZ CANAL
2	BUDDY HOLLY
3	JOHNNY RAY
4	PSYCHO
5	BARDOT
6	DACRON
7	PEYTON PLACE
9	ELIZABETH
11	NORTH KOREA
12	GRACE KELLY
13	ROCKEFELLER
15	JOSEPH STALIN
17	CHUBBY CHECKER
19	TOSCANINI
20	PROKOFIEV
21	JAMES DEAN
22	ALABAMA
23	BRIDGE ON THE RIVER KWAI
25	ROY COHN
26	HEMINGWAY
27	BRANDO
30	ROCK AROUND THE CLOCK
31	JOE MCCARTHY
36	DORIS DAY
38	DODGERS
39	BENHUR
40	DAVY CROCKETT
43	EISENHOWER
44	BAY OF PIGS
51	NASSER

-----------------------PAGE 70-----------------------
ACROSS

2	THE YOUNG ONES
5	HEADBANGERS
6	MONTY PYTHON
9	MINUTES
13	BROWN
14	THE BUGGLES
16	JACKSON
17	NINA
18	ALAN
20	REMOTE CONTROL
21	ANDY WARHOL
22	LIVE AID

DOWN

1	NEW JERSEY
2	THE CARS
3	THE BIG PICTURE
4	UNPLUGGED
7	PAT BENETAR
8	MADONNA
9	MARK
10	THE MONKEES
11	RAPS
12	QUINN
15	BON JOVI
19	AL TV

PAGE 69
ACROSS
1 MICHAEL JACKSON
2 RICK SPRINGFIELD
3 TINA TURNER
6 IRENE CARA
8 THE POLICE
10 WHAM
11 CULTURE CLUB
13 SIMPLE MINDS
15 VAN HALEN
18 POISON
19 WHITNEY HOUSTON
22 CYNDI LAUPER
23 BRUCE SPRINGSTEEN
24 GEORGE MICHAEL
25 PRINCE
26 JOAN JETT
28 MADONNA
29 SPANDAU BALLET
30 TEARS FOR FEARS
31 SURVIVOR
DOWN
1 MEN AT WORK
2 RICK ASTLEY
3 THE EURYTHMICS
4 TRACY CHAPMAN
5 AC/DC
7 JOURNEY
9 LIONEL RICHIE
12 PHIL COLLINS
14 DURAN DURAN
16 QUEEN
17 LIPPS INC
19 WHITESNAKE
20 THE BANGLES
21 THE GO-GOS
27 TOTO

PAGE 71
ACROSS
2 THE EVIL DEAD
5 COPS
6 FIRE
9 ANNIE
11 TECH-NOIR
13 PECK
15 FALCON
16 DUCK HUNT
18 AMARANTA
19 WAYNE GRETZKY
DOWN
1 DEVIL
3 APPLEBEES
4 BENDER
7 BOB HOSKINS
8 EL SALVADOR
9 ALIENS
10 WALKMAN
12 STIR CRAZY
14 CALGARY
17 TACO

PAGE 74
ACROSS
1 USA FOR AFRICA
5 FRANK ZAPPA
8 THE ENTITY
10 MR. HAND
14 GERANIUM
15 JELLY
17 BARF
18 HBO
19 RED DRAGON
DOWN
2 FERRET
3 CAPTAIN E.O.
4 DAKOTA
6 RELAX
7 STING
9 THE BURBS
11 BENSON
12 LAZER TAG
13 LEMOND
16 LOUVRE

PAGE 72
ACROSS
3 STEEL MAGNOLIAS
5 DINER
7 CREEPSHOW
8 HELLRAISER
13 THE FLY
15 HEATHERS
18 FIELD OF DREAMS
22 PLATOON
25 RISKY BUSINESS
31 ROMANCING THE STONE
33 DIRTY DANCING
35 COMMANDO
36 LETHAL WEAPON
37 THE THING
38 THE EMPIRE STRIKES BACK
DOWN
1 WALL STREET
2 SIXTEEN CANDLES
4 THE PURPLE ROSE OF CAIRO
6 WHO FRAMED ROGER RABBIT
9 SCARFACE
10 THEY LIVE
11 A CHRISTMAS STORY
12 THE UNTOUCHABLES
14 BROADCAST NEWS
16 MY FAVORITE YEAR
17 ROBOCOP
19 BACK TO THE FUTURE
20 CONAN THE BARBARIAN
21 SPLASH
23 THE LEGEND OF BILLY JEAN
24 FERRIS BUELLER'S DAY OFF
26 BEVERLY HILLS COP
27 MIDNIGHT RUN
28 LABYRINTH
29 HIGHLANDER
30 BULL DURHAM
32 DEAD POETS SOCIETY
34 MAJOR LEAGUE

PAGE 75
ACROSS
2 DESPERATELY SEEKING SUSAN
10 BATMAN
11 PURPLE RAIN
14 HIGHLANDER
16 THE COLOR OF MONEY
19 BACK TO THE FUTURE
20 THE BREAKFAST CLUB
21 THE JEWEL OF THE NILE
22 RUNNING SCARED
23 CHANCES ARE
24 LESS THAN ZERO
DOWN
1 COCKTAIL
3 SCROOGED
4 TOP GUN
5 FLASHDANCE
6 YENTL
7 ST. ELMO'S FIRE
8 THE LAST DRAGON
9 EARTH GIRLS ARE EASY
10 BEACHES
12 BEVERLY HILLS COP
13 RISKY BUSINESS
15 AT CLOSE RANGE
17 ROCKY IV
18 MANNEQUIN

PAGE 80
ACROSS
1 PHISH
5 COLON
6 PROZAC
9 FRIDAYS
11 COREY FELDMAN
12 STEREO
13 ATREYU
15 ALBANO
17 PIRATE
18 SALIERI
19 HAWK
DOWN
1 PINK FLOYD
2 CROSSROADS
3 DOLLY PARTON
4 PANAMA
7 BIG LEAGUE CHEW
8 MAD COW
10 FRANTIC
14 JARVIK
16 AKIRA

PAGE 76
ACROSS
2 TOXIC
4 MAC AND ME
7 MARBLES
10 GLADIATORS
11 MATLOCK
13 GALOOB
18 LEE IACOCCA
19 BEIRUT
20 DON BLUTH
DOWN
1 TALK RADIO
3 COSTCO
5 CAPER
6 JOHN FOGERTY
8 VALMONT
9 MICKEY
12 THE BEAR
14 OILERS
15 GROO
16 VELVET
17 SWATCH

PAGE 77
ACROSS
1 LEGEND
3 FLASH GORDON
7 DREAMSCAPE
9 BRAZIL
10 ENEMY MINE
12 BRAINSTORM
15 SCANNERS
16 BATTLE BEYOND THE STARS
19 PREDATOR
20 TRON
DOWN
2 ESCAPE FROM NEW YORK
4 DRAGONSLAYER
5 BACK TO THE FUTURE
6 THE ROAD WARRIOR
8 CLASH OF THE TITANS
11 HOWARD THE DUCK
13 EXPLORERS
14 BEETLEJUICE
17 OUTLAND
18 D.A.R.Y.L.

-------------------------PAGE 78-------------------------
ACROSS
1 HEAD OF THE CLASS
8 REMINGTON STEELE
11 THE A-TEAM
13 DYNASTY
16 SPENSER FOR HIRE
17 ALICE
22 BUFFALO BILL
23 FAMILY TIES
27 QUANTUM LEAP
29 COACH
32 THE SIMPSONS
35 PERFECT STRANGERS
36 THE COSBY SHOW
37 WHO'S THE BOSS?
38 PUNKY BREWSTER
39 THIRTYSOMETHING

DOWN
1 HOOPERMAN
2 AFTERMASH
3 HARDCASTLE AND MCCORMICK
4 MR. BELVEDERE
5 FANTASY ISLAND
6 THE GREATEST AMERICAN HERO
7 TRAPPER JOHN MD
9 POLICE SQUAD
10 ST. ELSEWHERE
12 HIGHWAY TO HEAVEN
14 MURDER, SHE WROTE
15 GIMME A BREAK
18 THE FALL GUY
19 T.J. HOOKER
20 MIAMI VICE
21 GROWING PAINS
22 BEAUTY AND THE BEAST
24 MATLOCK
25 THE WONDER YEARS
26 MAX HEADROOM
28 EMPTY NEST
30 CHINA BEACH
31 BAYWATCH
33 THE LOVE BOAT
34 MACGYVER

PAGE 81
ACROSS

1 THE BIG BRAWL
3 FIREWALKER
4 DIE HARD
7 ANY WHICH WAY YOU CAN
9 RAIDERS OF THE LOST ARK
12 BIG TROUBLE IN LITTLE CHINA
14 KING SOLOMON'S MINES
16 INVASION U.S.A.
17 UNCOMMON VALOR
18 BLIND FURY
19 THE LAST DRAGON

DOWN

1 THE LIVING DAYLIGHTS
2 BATMAN
5 SUDDEN IMPACT
6 SOUTHERN COMFORT
8 OCTOPUSSY
10 THE BIG RED ONE
11 COMMANDO
12 BLOODSPORT
13 RAW DEAL
15 TOP GUN

PAGE 86
ACROSS

1 AXEL F
4 KE HUY QUAN
5 LEGEND
6 CHAIR
8 ZOLTAR
9 JOSHUA
13 TOPOL
15 NINE INCH NAILS
16 BRUBAKER
17 EASY
18 WEREWOLF

DOWN

2 LARDASS
3 RANDY RHOADS
7 ZUUL
10 HOOSIERS
11 FERNANDO
12 I DON'T KNOW
14 OCTOPUSSY

PAGE 82
ACROSS

2 DON'T STOP BELIEVING
6 MAJOR TOM
7 MY PREROGATIVE
11 A TOWN CALLED MALICE
13 SHOUT
18 SAFETY DANCE
20 NEW SONG
21 MEXICAN RADIO
23 BOYS OF SUMMER
27 TAKE ON ME
28 NOTORIOUS
29 SAY SAY SAY
31 MISSING YOU
32 THE FLAME
33 BROKEN WINGS
34 WALK LIKE AN EGYPTIAN
35 BATDANCE
36 MICKEY
38 FAST CAR
39 BEDS ARE BURNING
40 CENTERFOLD
41 WOMAN IN LOVE
42 XANADU

DOWN

1 GIRLS JUST WANT TO HAVE FUN
3 TOM SAWYER
4 ADDICTED TO LOVE
5 ASHES TO ASHES
8 EYE OF THE TIGER
9 MAD ABOUT YOU
10 WEST END GIRLS
12 KARMA CHAMELEON
14 GHOSTBUSTERS
15 LOVE BITES
16 GOODY TWO SHOES
17 TAKE MY BREATH AWAY
19 SWEET CHILD O MINE
22 REBEL YELL
23 BLAME IT ON THE RAIN
24 COOL IT NOW
25 CARELESS WHISPER
26 LADY
30 SLEDGEHAMMER
37 ATOMIC

PAGE 84
ACROSS

2 BARBRA STREISAND
4 BILLY IDOL
7 KENNY ROGERS
10 BLONDIE
13 MIDNIGHT OIL
17 CHEAP TRICK
18 THE JAM
24 THE J. GEILS BAND
27 TONI BASIL
30 A-HA
33 PET SHOP BOYS
34 TEARS FOR FEARS
35 JOURNEY
37 BOBBY BROWN
38 MILLI VANILLI
39 MR. MISTER
40 DURAN DURAN
41 DEF LEPPARD

DOWN

1 JOHN WAITE
3 THE BANGLES
5 PRINCE
6 PETER SCHILLING
8 RUSH
9 BELINDA CARLISLE
10 BERLIN
11 RAY PARKER, JR.
12 ADAM ANT
14 WHAM
15 PETER GABRIEL
16 CULTURE CLUB
19 MEN WITHOUT HATS
20 NEW EDITION
21 DAVID BOWIE
22 OLIVIA NEWTON-JOHN
23 GUNS N ROSES
25 HOWARD JONES
26 WALL OF VOODOO
28 SURVIVOR
29 CYNDI LAUPER
31 ROBERT PALMER
32 TRACY CHAPMAN
36 DON HENLEY

PAGE 87
ACROSS

1	PEPSI
4	JAMES BROWN
6	BLACK ADDER
7	DUTCH
8	SOLID GOLD
14	ESKIMO
17	KEANU REEVES
18	KNIGHTRIDERS

DOWN

2	EPCOT
3	IRAN
5	NERDS
6	BROOKE SHIELDS
9	DUKE
10	EVIL ED
11	MILKEN
12	BOBSLED
13	FRATELLI
15	SHOWER
16	SPORTS

PAGE 91
ACROSS

2	CARS
6	DORF
9	MILLI VANILLI
10	BON SCOTT
13	EGYPT
14	HENRY V
15	QUEEN
17	COUNTDOWN
18	HEART
19	RAINBOW WARRIOR

DOWN

1	URBAN
3	ALEX WINTER
4	STRANGE BREW
5	WHAMMY
7	MUSIC
8	WHITNEY HOUSTON
11	TEMPEST
12	YELLO
16	MARIO

PAGE 88
ACROSS

2	MOONSTRUCK
3	MISSISSIPPI BURNING
6	RUTHLESS PEOPLE
7	MANNEQUIN
9	STEEL MAGNOLIAS
10	RED DAWN
11	THE ABYSS
16	THE SHINING
18	MY LEFT FOOT
22	THE MISSION
24	FLASHDANCE
30	DISORDERLIES
33	SHORT CIRCUIT
34	WEIRD SCIENCE
36	CONAN THE BARBARIAN
37	MYSTIC PIZZA
39	NEIGHBORS
40	PORKY'S
41	THE GOONIES
42	WORKING GIRL
43	ADVENTURES IN BABYSITTING

DOWN

1	JOHNNY DANGEROUSLY
4	BEETLEJUICE
5	RUNNING SCARED
8	FLETCH
12	TRON
13	THE FOG
14	OUT OF AFRICA
15	ENEMY MINE
17	WALL STREET
18	MY BODYGUARD
19	PLANES TRAINS AND AUTOMOBILES
20	BACK TO THE FUTURE
21	A CHRISTMAS STORY
23	SEEMS LIKE OLD TIMES
25	BEST DEFENSE
26	TRADING PLACES
27	FATAL ATTRACTION
28	HOWARD THE DUCK
29	HEAVEN'S GATE
31	BROADCAST NEWS
32	THE GREAT OUTDOORS
35	BRAZIL
38	PLATOON

PAGE 90
ACROSS

1	TIL TUESDAY
4	CHRIS DEBURGH
6	BALTIMORA
8	DON JOHNSON
9	WILL TO POWER
11	JACK WAGNER
12	AFTER THE FIRE
13	VIXEN
16	MIDNIGHT OIL
17	PAUL HARDCASTLE
21	PETER SCHILLING
25	WHEN IN ROME
26	MATTHEW WILDER
27	EDDIE MURPHY
28	MARY JANE GIRLS
30	ROCKWELL
31	GENERAL PUBLIC
32	NENEH CHERRY

DOWN

1	THE OUTFIELD
2	NU-SHOOZ
3	JERMAINE STEWART
5	MARTIKA
6	BOY MEETS GIRL
7	MICHAEL PENN
10	THE POWER STATION
14	BOYS DON'T CRY
15	FALCO
18	ANIMOTION
19	JAN HAMMER
20	ALANNAH MYLES
22	THE CHURCH
23	NIK KERSHAW
24	LIMAHL
28	M|A|R|R|S
29	J.J. FAD

PAGE 92
ACROSS
1 THREE AMIGOS
2 TOP SECRET
4 AIRPLANE!
6 LOST IN AMERICA
9 UNCLE BUCK
10 THE MONEY PIT
12 SPIES LIKE US
13 OVERBOARD
14 BLIND DATE
15 TRADING PLACES
16 THE CANNONBALL RUN
17 HEATHERS
18 DRAGNET
DOWN
1 TURNER AND HOOCH
3 THE BREAKFAST CLUB
4 A FISH CALLED WANDA
5 THE 'BURBS
7 BACHELOR PARTY
8 BETTER OFF DEAD
11 STRIPES

PAGE 93
ACROSS
3 BLOOD DINER
4 THE KEEP
9 ELECTRIC DREAMS
10 THE KEEP
13 BASKET CASE
15 THE ICE PIRATES
18 NIGHT SHIFT
19 THE PRIVATE EYES
20 ON THE RIGHT TRACK
21 BLOOD BEACH
DOWN
1 MIRACLE MILE
2 SOUL MAN
5 UNDER THE RAINBOW
6 CLOAK AND DAGGER
7 OH, HEAVENLY DOG
8 ZAPPED
11 STREET TRASH
12 SOCIETY
14 HEARTBEEPS
16 THE TOY
17 KIDCO

PAGE 94
ACROSS
2 NICOLAS CAGE
4 NICK NOLTE
9 DREW BARRYMORE
11 DANIEL STERN
13 MICHAEL J. FOX
14 MEL BROOKS
17 HOLLY HUNTER
18 JAMES EARL JONES
19 TOM HANKS
20 CHUCK NORRIS
22 TOM CRUISE
24 KEVIN COSTNER
27 MATT DILLON
28 LIAM NEESON
29 COREY FELDMAN
32 ROBIN WILLIAMS
35 DANNY GLOVER
36 GLENN CLOSE
38 RUTGER HAUER
40 JOHNNY DEPP
42 JAMES WOODS
43 MICHAEL DOUGLAS
44 MATTHEW BRODERICK
45 JOHN CANDY
DOWN
1 JOHN HURT
3 GENE HACKMAN
5 CHARLIE SHEEN
6 VAL KILMER
7 BRUCE WILLIS
8 JEFF GOLDBLUM
10 MEL GIBSON
12 MEG RYAN
15 BILLY CRYSTAL
16 ALEC BALDWIN
21 DANIEL DAY LEWIS
23 MOLLY RINGWALD
25 CLINT EASTWOOD
26 BURT REYNOLDS
30 ROBERT DOWNEY, JR.
31 CHARLES BRONSON
33 MICHAEL CAINE
34 CHEVY CHASE
37 PATRICK SWAYZE
39 JON CRYER
41 CHER

PAGE 96
ACROSS
3 TERROR IN THE AISLES
5 THE SHINING
6 WITCHBOARD
8 BAD TASTE
12 VAMPIRE'S KISS
14 LIFEFORCE
15 THE HAND
16 KILLER KLOWNS FROM OUTER SPACE
18 THE HUNGER
19 INVADERS FROM MARS
20 NOMADS
DOWN
1 FRIGHT NIGHT
2 CHILDS PLAY
4 THE MONSTER SQUAD
5 THE EVIL DEAD
7 THE BELIEVERS
9 THE BRIDE
10 THE FUNHOUSE
11 GHOST STORY
13 PUMPKINHEAD
17 CUJO

PAGE 97
ACROSS
1 STRANGE INVADERS
3 RUNAWAY
5 INNERSPACE
7 SWAMP THING
10 COCOON
11 DUNE
12 VIBES
14 RETURN TO OZ
15 ALIEN FROM L.A.
17 FLIGHT OF THE NAVIGATOR
18 THE ABYSS
19 THE DARK CRYSTAL
DOWN
2 THE LAST STARFIGHTER
4 NIGHT OF THE COMET
6 WINGS OF DESIRE
8 THE STUFF
9 DEADLY FRIEND
13 STARMAN
16 AKIRA

PUZZLED BY THE 80s 2 – CROSSWORD BOOGALOO

--------------------------PAGE 98------------------------

ACROSS

2	THE LITTLE MERMAID
5	THE MEANING OF LIFE
7	ROXANNE
14	THE COLOR OF MONEY
16	RED DAWN
17	WARGAMES
18	CLUE
19	LITTLE SHOP OF HORRORS
27	THE LAST STARFIGHTER
28	LABYRINTH
29	THE SHINING
34	THREE AMIGOS
36	THE ABYSS
37	FLETCH
38	ROBOCOP
40	DIE HARD
41	WEIRD SCIENCE
42	MAJOR LEAGUE
43	DIRTY ROTTEN SCOUNDRELS
45	BULL DURHAM

DOWN

1	TRON
3	ANGEL HEART
4	SCROOGED
5	THE BIG CHILL
6	LETHAL WEAPON
8	STRIPES
9	HELLRAISER
10	YOUNG GUNS
11	PEE WEE'S BIG ADVENTURE
12	PRETTY IN PINK
13	DANGEROUS LIAISONS
15	THE OUTSIDERS
20	THE WORLD ACCORDING TO GARP
21	EXCALIBUR
22	MY FAVORITE YEAR
23	CONAN THE BARBARIAN
24	SIXTEEN CANDLES
25	CLASH OF THE TITANS
26	ROMANCING THE STONE
30	A FISH CALLED WANDA
31	GLORY
32	FIELD OF DREAMS
33	THE SECRET OF NIMH
35	THE LOST BOYS
39	VACATION
44	UHF

PAGE 100

ACROSS

1	FRIGHT NIGHT
5	HEATHERS
10	LUCAS
15	DIRTY DANCING
17	SIXTEEN CANDLES
19	THE BREAKFAST CLUB
20	DREAM A LITTLE DREAM
21	SUMMER SCHOOL
22	FOOTLOOSE

DOWN

2	THE KARATE KID
3	VALLEY GIRL
4	THE LOST BOYS
6	RED DAWN
7	WEIRD SCIENCE
8	SAY ANYTHING
9	THE OUTSIDERS
10	LICENSE TO DRIVE
11	PRETTY IN PINK
12	CAN'T BUY ME LOVE
13	BETTER OFF DEAD
14	RISKY BUSINESS
16	TEEN WOLF
18	CLASS

ALSO AVAILABLE

PUZZLED BY THE 80s - Gnarly Word Searches, Bogus Crosswords, Radical Cryptograms, and More
The 80s were a time of massive economic and geopolitical changes. But we're not getting into any of the serious stuff! Instead, dive into puzzles focusing on the pop culture of the 1980s - the movies, the music, the TV shows, the fads, and more! This book contains 85 80's-themed puzzles like word searches, crosswords, cryptograms, and anagrams as well as all the solutions.

MOVIE QUOTE CRYPTOGRAMS - 500+ Quotes From the Last 90 Years of Cinema
This book contains over 500 quotes from movies, ranging from the earliest of talkies to the most recent blockbusters. Some of the quotes are very well known (say, Casablanca's "Of all the gin joints..." quote), but many of them delve deeper into the movie - it won't be as easy as figuring out the title and immediately knowing the whole quote. It should be noted that these aren't all just one liners! Many of the quotes are from monologues or extended dialogue sequences. Some take up an entire page!

WORD NERD USA - United States of America-Themed Word Search Puzzles
There are plenty of words to love in this word search puzzle book. Each puzzle is themed to the United States of America. There are puzzles for each state and U.S. territory. There are also puzzles for American originated subjects, like food, television, movies, and even animals that are all from the USA. The mega puzzles at the end of the book extend your fun.
This book offers large print word search puzzles that are easy on your eyes.
 Even the font for each puzzle was selected to help prevent eye strain.

BIRD SEARCH USA - A Word Search Book for Bird Lovers
Birds are everywhere. Even when you can't see them, you can hear them. The United States of America enjoys a wide variety of wild birds. This book offers two large print word search puzzles for each U.S. state. These are birds you could actually find in the state. Look for the italicized bird in the word bank - this is the official state bird. As you work through this word search puzzle book, you'll notice how some birds appear in states next to each other and in states several hundred miles away. It's fun to see how birds get around. You'll also notice how popular certain species are for official state bird.

HORRIBLE PUZZLES - Horror Crosswords, Word Searches, and More
Contained within this book you'll find 90 puzzles - words searches, crosswords, cryptograms, anagrams, and even a few goofy ones just to keep things interesting. The subject of every one of these is horror - be it horror films, horror literature, horror television, even horror video games. We cover authors, directors, tag lines from posters, famous (and infamous) quotes, and more. Interspersed amongst the puzzles is commentary that briefly tries to explain how the subjects featured in the puzzles fit into the grand scheme of the horror genre.

PUZZLED BY THE 70s - Groovy Word Searches, Radical Crosswords, Stellar Cryptograms,
This book takes all the major pop culture milestones - all the cinematic trends, all the musical stylings, and puts them all into a blender. Featuring dozens of word search puzzles, crossword puzzles, cryptograms, anagrams, kriss kross puzzles, and even period-correct logic puzzles, They're all here. Each puzzle is accompanied by short write-ups that point out what was in the zeitgeist at the time (such as which films moviegoers were flocking to, or, which albums were critically acclaimed).